Developing a
Coaching Business

Coaching in Practice series

The aim of this series is to help coaching professionals gain a broader understanding of the challenges and issues they face in coaching, enabling them to make the leap from being a 'good-enough' coach to an outstanding one. This series is an essential aid for both the novice coach eager to learn how to grow a coaching practice, and the more experienced coach looking for new knowledge and strategies. Combining theory with practice, it provides a comprehensive guide to becoming successful in this rapidly expanding profession.

Forthcoming titles:

Hayes: *NLP Coaching*
Bluckert: *Psychological Dimensions to Coaching*
Hay: *Reflective Practice and Supervision for Coaches*
Vaughan Smith: *Therapist into Coach*

Developing a Coaching Business

Jenny Rogers

Open University Press

Open University Press
McGraw-Hill Education
McGraw-Hill House
Shoppenhangers Road
Maidenhead
Berkshire
England
SL6 2QL

email: enquiries@openup.co.uk
world wide web: www.openup.co.uk

and Two Penn Plaza, New York, NY 10121-2289, USA

First published 2006

A catalogue record of this book is available from the British Library

ISBN-10: 0 335 22049 5 (pb) 0 335 22050 9 (hb)
ISBN-13: 978 0335 22049 6 (pb) 978 0335 22050 2 (hb)

Library of Congress Cataloging-in-Publication Data
CIP data applied for

Typeset by YHT Ltd, London
Printed in Poland by OzGraf S.A.
www.polskabook.pl

Contents

Series Preface

The coaching world is expanding. A profession that was largely unknown a decade ago is now an attractive second career for increasing numbers of people looking for new ways of growing their interest in the development of people. Some observers reckon that the number of new coaches joining the market is doubling every year.

Yet while there are many books which cater for the beginner coach, including my own book, also published by Open University Press, *Coaching Skills: A Handbook*, there are relatively few which explore and deepen more specialist aspects of the role. That is the purpose of this series. It is called *Coaching in Practice* because the aim is to unite theory and practice in an accessible way. The books are short, designed to be easily understood without in any way compromising on the integrity of the ideas they explore. All are written by senior coaches with, in every case, many years of hands-on experience.

This series is for you if you are undertaking or completing your coaching training and perhaps in the early stages of the unpredictability, pleasures and dilemmas that working with actual clients brings. Now that you have passed the honeymoon stage, you may have begun to notice the limitations of your approaches and knowledge. You are eager for more information and guidance. You probably know that it is hard to make the leap between being a good-enough coach and an outstanding one. You are thirsty for more help and challenge. You may also be one of the many people still contemplating a career in coaching. If so, these books will give you useful direction on many of the issues which preoccupy, perplex and delight the working coach.

That is where I hope you will find the *Coaching in Practice* series so useful.

Other titles in this series are about hands-on work with clients. This one is about the equally important topic of how you build a coaching business. Being a coach means that you are in effect running a small business, but what does this mean in practice? How is the coaching market developing and what are the implications for any coach? How should you sustain yourself while you are building your business? Which promotional activities really pay off and which are waste of time and money? Coaching programmes are typically short and finite so it is essential to have a steady stream of new clients, but how do you find them, and even more importantly, how do you sell with integrity? This book aims to give you practical guidance on all of these topics—and more, from someone who has been there and done it.

Introduction

Most of the coaches I have trained are far happier about developing their coaching skills than they are about dealing with the business side of their new profession. If you are one of them, then this is your book.

I have aimed it at five groups:

The novice coach starting out with high hopes and eager to learn how to grow a coaching practice, whether as a life coach, a specialist coach of some sort, or an executive coach.

More experienced coaches who already know that being a brilliant coach is not enough and want to learn where they are already doing the right thing and what practical strategies they might try in order to find new clients more quickly.

People running a coaching service inside organizations – they face most of the same issues, albeit in a different context.

Consultants and other independent operators interested in developing a coaching business and who already have useful experience of what is involved.

Therapists and counsellors who may or may not be considering coaching as a field, but who see that they, too, are running a business and want to learn how to do it more effectively.

This is not a book of academic business theory. It is not about how to do coaching – there are plenty of other books on that, including one I have written myself. Nor is it competing with the many books aimed at small-business owners and already on the bookshops' shelves about how to do sales forecasts, double-entry bookkeeping or calculate your VAT.

I make no promises about quick fixes because there are none. Nothing in this book is based on hype or silly pledges about getting rich in 100 days. Instead, I have based the book on sixteen successful years as a coach myself, training hundreds of other coaches, supervising around a dozen beginner coaches at any one time and observing their subsequent professional progress with keen interest. A business that started as just me is now a much bigger concern and in writing the book I have drawn substantially not just on my own experience but also on the experience of colleagues. We have tried everything in it and all the recommendations are drawn from knowledge of what works.

My purpose in writing it has been to pass on to you the many practical lessons we have learnt, not least to save you making the same mistakes, some of them expensive, that we made along the way. Coaching is a terrific way to earn a living, but you will have to accept that in committing to it, you are also committing to running a business. Like any other small business it all starts with being clear about what you offer to your market, understanding what that market wants and will pay for, promoting it skilfully and then selling it with flair and enjoyment. I'm not going to pretend that everything we do is now error-free because it isn't, or that it is not a constant battle – a pleasant one most of the time – to keep ahead of the game, because it is. Our field is competitive and becoming more so by the day. But the rewards when you get there are wonderful.

The task ahead may seem daunting if you are brand new to most of this thinking. Perhaps that is because it is indeed daunting, but I would rather help you be realistic about what is involved, especially since I encounter many coaches who see their new career as some kind of Elysium which will solve every career and personal problem. However, I have also indicated at the end of each chapter what the essentials are and which investments in your time and money are more optional – perhaps for a later stage in the development of your business.

If you care about coaching, then it matters to run a thriving practice. How to do it is what this book is about.

1 Coaching as a Business

You go into coaching because you positively love what you do. You are buoyed up by the prospect of being able to practise your craft and the magnificent freedom from boring meetings or tedious organizational politicking that you anticipate enjoying.

Yet it's clear from the US and from anecdotal UK evidence that the great majority of coaches struggle to make a living. They have merely swapped one kind of stress for another. For instance, fewer than one third of all first year coaches in the US manage to find more than 10 clients. Only 9 per cent of American coaches are earning a comfortable income from coaching. We also know from both British and US sources that the failure rate of all small businesses is phenomenally high. Only a minority survive their first four years.

There are two overall reasons why coaches fail to achieve their ambitions. The first is poor-quality coaching. If you are no good at the basics of your profession then you will miss out on one of the main ways that successful coaches get business: repeat orders and word of mouth recommendation. Improving your coaching technique is beyond the scope of this book. Rigorous training which includes candid assessment as part of a gold-standard accreditation process is your best bet here.

The second reason for failure is not understanding that, like it or not, you are running a business. That is the subject of this book: building a successful practice and avoiding the common traps. You can't be half-hearted. Just as you can't be a little bit pregnant, you can't be sort-of enthusiastic about running a business. If you are thinking that coaching could be a nice hobby while you live off your handsome pension, or that your real love is your garden – and you will do the odd bit of coaching to subsidize the exotic plants that otherwise you couldn't afford – think again. It won't work. You have to be committed. If you're not, put this book back on the shelf now.

Six essential foundations of success

1 Seriousness, focus and stamina

This is the first principle for any successful small business. Accept that you are in it for the long haul. It will take you minimally eighteen months to develop a truly profitable coaching business and the majority of coaches will find that it takes longer even than that. Most of this time will be spent in the long slog to let the world know what you offer and then to persuade your target clients to buy.

It's true that there is a small minority of coaches who appear to have been successful from the start. But when you look closely at their experience you will see that virtually all of them had laid prudent foundations long before they launched themselves. This was very true for one of our Diploma candidates.

> *Donald*
> I was employed in a large pharmaceutical company as part of their global Human Resources (HR) team. My work was extremely well paid, but I was spending all my time on planes and often I'd have to pinch myself to remind myself which country I was in. It was phenomenally tiring and I was constantly homesick. I realized that what I really loved was the one-to-one aspects of my work and that another name for what I was doing was coaching.
>
> I made it clear to my boss that I could offer significant benefit to the organization as a coach and after getting the Diploma, began building my practice internally. From the start I aimed at specific goals: in my first year it was to complete 300 hours of coaching. Although it was only one part of my job, after two years I began to get more referrals than I could cope with and decided to take the plunge and go independent. I had already been buying bits of computer kit and learning how to use them. I persuaded my employer to let me access the typical internal client I was targeting and also to give me a modest start-off contract. Although I began where I was known, my aim was steadily to broaden out and to get clients to recommend me to others outside the sector.
>
> As a result, I've always been busy and my launch happened so smoothly it surprised even me. Other coaches often tell me I was lucky, but I don't think it was luck really – just clarity and determination. I knew early on where I was going.

2 Be clear that you really do want to be self-employed

Earlier in my career, I worked as a television producer at the BBC. I remember the awe I felt when colleagues took what seemed like the enormous risk of leaving to go independent. At the time I had young children and a large mortgage. I needed the predictability and certainty of working in an organization where the monthly pay-cheque came in regardless. Yet only a decade later, I found myself itching to tell my boss that I was leaving to set up my own coaching and consulting business. In the end the compulsion to do it became overwhelming. But the time and personal circumstances had to be right. By that stage, the mortgage had shrunk to manageable size and the end of parenting was in sight. It should always be a positive decision, not one that feels as if it's the best of a bad job, or a transition while you look for a proper job. When you choose self-employment, that is your proper job. Anything else is just playing around and is unlikely to lead to success, as this would-be coach found:

> *Martin*
>
> I was a casualty of yet another reorganization. I was fed up with it. I decided on what was probably a bit of a whim that I wanted to set up my own business as a coach. As a single gay man I have no dependants and there was only the mortgage and the dogs to feed. I'd had a fantastic coach myself as part of an earlier leaving package and it seemed like a wonderfully enjoyable way of earning a living, helping people and getting to know them. I enrolled for a distance learning course on coaching and went to one or two days of workshops, and it all seemed great. I thought people would somehow just find me, especially the people in my old company. I wince now when I think of it. I discovered later that people thought I was too much part of what had failed.
>
> I priced myself at the same rate as my own coach, thinking that I probably had very similar skills, but people just wouldn't pay those rates. It was all a horrible experience. The worst of it was that I got lonely and I began to hate sitting at home. Those dogs did a lot of listening! After six months I'd earned a pathetic amount and I panicked.
>
> I decided I'd have to look for proper employment again, but by then the economy was in recession and it was more difficult than I'd thought. I believe employers saw me as neither one thing nor the other – if I was running a business then why was I looking for a job? My morale was at rock bottom when I saw a job advertised at a lot below what I had been earning previously. I got it but it doesn't really feel right. I still have a long-term ambition to coach but I realize I've got to approach it differently next time.

In Martin's story there are a lot of familiar erroneous assumptions. First, there is his romantic view of coaching as *helping and getting to know* people. Coaching is not romantic. It's a business – an enjoyable one when it's going well, but a business none the less. It's less about *helping* people than it is about *working* with them. Then he rushed into coaching as a reaction to losing his job rather than preparing carefully after a measured decision. He had not made a realistic assessment about the psychological side of self-employment. His training programme was sketchy and his business skills elementary.

Finally, and fatally, he was unprepared for the perseverance necessary to establish a business and in his panic split his energies between a job hunt and endeavouring to make his business work.

Try completing this questionnaire. It gives you a chance to consider your initial responses to the whole idea. Essentially it's about the balance between how much you would like the autonomy that self-employment brings and how much you would fear the lack of stability and predictability that is also part of life for most self-employed people.

Tick the column that represents how much you would like any of these features of the self-employed life.

Key: 3 = an important factor for you, 2 = a moderately important factor, 1 = a relatively minor factor.

Yes, I'd enjoy the possibility of this	3	2	1
Only doing the work I want to do			
Managing my own working day			
Freedom from organizational politics			
Not having to spend time in pointless meetings			
Selling to clients			
Getting a direct relationship between activity and income			
Setting my own targets			
Being able to blend work and home			
Working alone			
Working with the associates I choose and really like			
Getting a variety of tasks			
Working with a range of organizations			
Being potentially able to increase my income from its present level			
Being able to use all my abilities			
Choosing exactly how hard I want to work			
Total score for potential enjoyment factors			

Now do the same for this list – the factors that may be discouragers and a disincentive to self-employment.

Key: 3 = a serious disincentive, 2 = a mild disincentive, 1 = a minor disincentive.

Yes, I could find this a discourager/disincentive	3	2	1
Getting potentially too narrow in my focus through lack of contact with colleagues			
Missing the legitimate opportunity to get away from domestic concerns during the day			
Missing the gossip of organizational life			
Missing 'busywork' – low-key chores such as meetings which offer pleasant and legitimate excuses to avoid more demanding work			
Having to sell myself and fearing rejection			
Missing the predictability of a regular salary			
Getting sloppy through having no imposed targets			
Wanting a clear separation between work and home			
Missing 'hanging loose' with colleagues, feeling lonely on my own			
Having to do and be everything – post-collector, customer-carer, secretary ...			
Missing the enjoyment and security of knowing one organization in depth			
Missing having a boss who can coach and support me – having to do this for myself			
Worrying about whether I know enough to run every aspect of a business			
Knowing that work flow can sometimes be unpredictable – 'feast or famine' and fearing having little control over it			
Overworking out of fear that the next job will be the last			
Total score for potential disincentives/discouragers			

There are 15 items in each list.

How do your totals compare? Are there some items in each list that you rate **_super-important_**? If so, give them each an extra two points.

What is the balance between the two lists? How does this leave you feeling now?

If you feel negative, then you probably need to concentrate on finding work as an employee. If you feel positive or still interested enough to continue exploration, then carry on reading this book to find out more.

3 Target your niche

The barriers to entry are low in the coaching world. You could, if you really wanted to, start out with just your home phone, a computer and a few dozen simple business cards. This is not desirable, but it is possible. Some observers have reckoned that the number of new coaches entering the market is doubling every year. This is because, at first sight, coaching looks easy. All of these are entering coaching currently:

People who have been made redundant. They hope that because they have been successful as managers or experts in their field, the world will seek out their wisdom as coaches.

The big accounting consultancies, management consultancies and some of the major executive search (head-hunting) firms who have realized that coaching could carry them through recession or economic slowdown.

Training organizations who see coaching as a way of adding strength and depth to their market offer.

People making a positive career-change choice to enter coaching. They may have left consultancies or training companies because they believe they can earn more money solo.

Counsellors and therapists who now understand that coaching and counselling are close cousins. They realize that coaches earn more and many think they will turn their hand to a different market.

The only way to survive in this competitive environment is to target what you offer. This means clarifying what you offer (*everything* is not acceptable as an answer) and to whom (*everyone* is not acceptable as an answer). The biggest single mistake that most novice coaches make is to aim too broadly. When you don't differentiate yourself you make success many times more difficult. How to do this is the focus of Chapter 2.

4 Embrace the world of selling

Selling has a bad press as a word. We associate it with the clumsy, scripted intrusions of the call centre work-horse, desperate to tell you that you have 'won' a competition for which you never entered. We think about the bullying of the salesperson who coerces a naïve young couple into buying the kitchen they cannot afford, or the oppressive attention of the upmarket boutique saleswoman who is working on commission. Most of us have fallen for these tactics at some time.

One trap is that failing to make a sale can be attributed to factors other than our own selling skills. I have heard novice coaches attribute their disappointments to all of these:

> *The client was too stupid to recognize my calibre.*
> *It was all a set-up and a fix.*
> *They went for the cheapest because they're too mean to hire the best.*
> *They went for the most expensive because of the snob value.*
> *My competitor used dirty tricks to get the work.*

Most coaches are totally unused to professional failure. We tend to have passed our exams, achieved regular promotions painlessly and acquired important-sounding titles which earned us pleasant offices and an agreeable sense of status. If you enter coaching from the world of the public sector then you have the further shock of moving from a spending organization to one (your own) where income has to be earned before it can be spent. Many of us have also come from worlds where success is actually a bit of a fluffy concept, too vague for robust measurement, or where there is remarkably little direct, candid feedback on our performance. This could not be more different from the world of running a small business where the feedback loop is brutally short and direct.

Many beginner coaches would love to believe the myth that good work will sell itself. They wait for people to find their way to their door. Or else they succumb to the fantasy that where you have a dream, your dream will come true just because you want it to. Or that the absolute purity of your intention will somehow convey itself to your market and virtue will be its own reward.

Another version of the same trap is to assume that your existing reputation and network will be big enough to produce a steady stream of clients. That is unlikely, as this coach's rueful account shows:

Sara

When I look back I made every mistake in the book. I had left my organization with a high reputation and a lot of goodwill. I wrote to everyone I knew well in it, letting them know about my new career and address. I had a lot of confidence in my ability as a coach and was eager to get on with the work. I just expected the phone to ring but of course it didn't. I joined the Institute of Directors and did set up a few lunches there with former colleagues. These were pleasant, but never created any work.

I see now that my network was just too small to generate enough clients quickly. I hated the idea of selling myself, especially when it came to naming a fee. I didn't realize that I had to put in a huge amount of spade work before I could do the thing I really wanted, which was just do the coaching. I know now that you can't just be a coach – you've got to be Sales Director and Chief Accountant, as well as the person who goes to the post office or commissions the email system. I was still determined to do it, but I had to find myself a low-stress part-time job in a gym to sustain me while I put in all the real preparatory work I should have done in the first place. Eventually this paid off, but it was tough.

If, like Sara, you have a morbid fear of selling, remind yourself of this: no salesperson in the world makes the sale every time. Failure is part of the game. The challenge is to reduce its frequency.

Another positive and enjoyable challenge with selling is to realize that you can do it with the same integrity that you bring to your actual coaching. You will not find tricks or high-pressure techniques in this book. Like anyone who sells with integrity, there will be times when you draw back from an easy sale. There will also be times when you decide that your dislike of a client organization, and of the values you see in action around it, will make it impossible for you to work with its people. This is one part of what selling with integrity means. The other is that you only sell what clients both want and need at a price they can afford. There is nothing intrinsically morally flawed about kitchen fitments, uPVC windows, time-share holidays or expensive fashion clothing. The negative associations come from the way they are sold. You have to believe in the quality of what you do and you have to believe in its value. As the US sales guru Alan Wiess constantly points out, your first sale is to yourself. If you don't believe you, why should anyone else?

Remember, too, that you have probably been doing a lot more selling in your previous roles than you realize. Have you had to persuade people to take one path rather than another? Have you had to find a home for a new idea? In that case you have been selling ideas, and the same principles that applied to success there will work when you are selling coaching. It is true that some coaches find it easier to sell an objective entity – or even someone else – than the personal feel it can have when you are selling yourself. But even here, many people find an unexpected relish in the task:

> *Clive*
> Part of being a good coach is to know yourself and I came to realize, after lots of denial, that I am pretty competitive. And also that I do enjoy selling, whatever my initial bashfulness. For instance, I have always loved selling at car boots or school fêtes and now on eBay. There's satisfaction in seeing someone walk away with something you have sold them at a car boot just as there is pleasure in landing a new client. Personally I think all we coaches need to start enjoying it and not feeling it's something to be ashamed of.

Even if you were giving away your coaching – which, by the way, is an excellent way of establishing your practice, see later – you will still have to sell both the benefits of coaching to your client and why you are the person to deliver them.

Without sales effort there will be no coaching and without coaching there will be no income.

The solution is selling with integrity: the topic I explore in Chapter 5.

5 Be realistic about start-up costs

There are three sets of cost you will need to consider for your first year:

office and office equipment;

immediate launch costs;

ongoing expenses associated with marketing.

New coaches tend to know about the first two and may seriously underestimate the costs of the third. Remember, too, that one of the main causes of small-business failure is under-capitalization. Avoiding this through careful financial planning is one of the ways to establish a thriving business.

Office and office equipment

Most new coaches start from home. It is cheap, simple and may have the additional attraction of fulfilling part of your dream – a wish to get a better work–life balance, see your family more, enjoy your pets, spend less time on tiresome commuting – and so on. But think carefully about this. Unless you propose to do the majority of your coaching by phone – extremely rare in the UK – you will need to have a room which fulfils these criteria:

flexible email program with spam and junk-mail filters and the best virus-protection program available at the time. It will also pay to buy a notebook or laptop computer so that you have a portable office wherever you go. Remember that computers are consumable items, not investments, and need replacing regularly.

Buy a robust back-up system for your computer files. In my early years as a coach, a computer failure put my hard drive at risk and with it all the handout material I had developed: the intellectual heart of my business. Several years later, and more savvy, I was relieved that our back-up system was safely in another building when our server was sabotaged by a burglar.

Invest in a printer–copier–scanner–fax.

Buy wireless broadband internet access.

Telephony

If you are working from home you need a separate phone line with its own voicemail. You will not want to have your children taking your messages or your clients to hear the cheery voicemail you have for your friends and family. You may want to buy a simple small-business phone system which gives the caller three or four options: how to contact you on your mobile; how to get information about your services; how to leave a message. You must also have a mobile or a BlackBerry and it needs to be kept switched on whenever possible.

Although it is unlikely that you will be doing all your coaching by phone, you will probably do some of it that way. A hands-free phone and headset will spare you the aching neck and shoulders that come from crouching over your desk for too long with a conventional handset.

Other start-up costs

There are some one-off costs associated with starting off. I will say more about how to choose the content and approach of your promotional materials in Chapter 3, but for now, note that you will need:

Stationery: headed paper; compliment slips; business cards; envelopes. You will need a corporate identity and must get this professionally designed. The most important piece of stationery is the business card and you should print enough to be able to give out at least 1000 in your first year.

Professional advice. Initially you can get a lot of this free at any of the banks which have branches big enough to support a business adviser. But sooner or later you will need the advice of a bookkeeper or accountant. When I started out I kept my accountant for an initial advisory consultation and then for the yearly tax return. The rest of the time, I used the services of a wonderfully efficient friend who specializes in bookkeeping for small, creative businesses. This continued until the time a few years later when she sacked me on the grounds that the company was now far too big for her to cope with, and told me in the nicest possible way that we needed to get a proper accountant to look after our books. That accountant now not only looks after the books but also administers our pay roll and many other useful tasks, but this was definitely not necessary at the outset.

You do need good up-to-date advice about tax and money. If you don't have a friendly local bookkeeper, then try Tax Assist, a franchised operation specializing in advising businesses too small to need a Certified or Chartered Accountant (www.taxassist.co.uk). Any of these sources will advise you about the best legal status for your business: a complex and ever-changing balance of how to minimize your tax obligations and protect your personal or business assets. Essentially the differences are that a Limited Company will protect your personal assets if you run into financial problems and will also look more serious to your market. The disadvantage is that you may pay more tax, depending on your turnover. If you opt for Sole Trader status there are considerable tax advantages, again depending on turnover, but if you run into serious debt problems, your home and other assets could be at risk.

Insurance. You need Professional Indemnity Insurance to protect you against being sued. This policy is usually obtainable cheaply from any professional association to which you belong. Failing that, any insurance company will give you a quote. If you are using your home as an office, you will also need Public Liability Insurance.

A website is a necessity. Again, professional help will repay the relatively small initial investment (page 52).

Professional associations. It is useful to think about two separate kinds of organization: the sort where you can keep your professional knowledge up to date and network with others in the same field and the sort where you can meet potential clients. Don't confuse the two.

Ongoing marketing costs

This is the big hidden cost of your first year and most of it is time. Accept now that you will be spending a lot of your energy phoning people, writing to them, emailing, lunching them, going to network events, writing articles and speaking at meetings. You are doing this to gain the recognition which will eventually bring you clients. The cash-out part of it is in entertaining and events fees. It is also sensible to set aside a budget for ongoing training and development. The rest – and this is by far the biggest part – is in how you support yourself while you are building that vital recognition. Here is how a number of other successful coaches have done it:

- Negotiating a part-time contract with their existing employer, either for a set number of days a year, or more frequently a two- or three-day week. This keeps some reliable income flowing while leaving enough time to build the new business.

Upsides: reduces financial anxiety; allows you to find out if you really do like the world of small business and coaching as much as you think you will.

Downsides: can create conflicts of interest. May risk the employer feeling used. May leave the coach feeling pulled all ways and therefore losing focus.

- Running a complementary activity side by side with coaching. This is probably the best option if you have other skills for which people are already paying money. Most of the successful coaches I know do in fact continue to work this way. Their facilitation or training work finds them coaching clients and vice versa. If you are already an established counsellor, trainer, or consultant, then this is the natural way to go. For more on this, see Chapter 4.

Upsides: steady income stream; natural way of generating new coaching clients.

Downsides: few, but there is a small risk that the other work could fill too much space, leaving you with little time to develop your coaching business.

- Relying on a partner to be the breadwinner.

Upsides: when cleanly negotiated makes the new business an exciting joint enterprise; keeps it in the family.

Downsides: spreading the anxiety about money; alters the balance of power in the relationship; partner may not always be as willing as he/she seemed initially; going without former luxuries may create tension.

- Bank loan or second mortgage.

Upsides: a business proposition and if the bank or mortgage company is convinced then you have already cleared your first hurdle. Reduces immediate worry about money.

Downsides: the risk of failure and the consequences for your entire household if that were to happen.

You will notice that crossing your fingers and hoping for the best is not on this list. That's because it doesn't work.

6 Train and prepare

The world of 'real' jobs in big organizations is often thought to be tough, competitive, harsh and unforgiving. So it may be. But it does have many advantages. When your computer goes wrong, there will be a Help Desk to fix it. Your email is set up for you. When the photocopier doesn't work, there will always be a better informed colleague who can sort out the paper trays. Your mobile will be upgraded for you. People come to collect your post. There is a restaurant, or a range of pleasant sandwich bars nearby. There may even be someone to fuss over you and manage your diary, book your travel or prettify your PowerPoint presentations.

It is unlikely that you will have any of this in the early days of developing a coaching business. Build your self-sufficiency in these matters, ideally before you leave conventional employment. Develop and deepen your keyboarding and computer skills. Learn to use as many of the desk-top publishing packages as you can (though see Chapter 3 about recognizing the limits of your own expertise as a designer). Find out what email can really do.

You must invest in coaching skills training. When I first began as a coach no one ever asked me whether I had any training, which was just as well as the answer would have been *no*. That was because there wasn't any and the market for coaching was rudimentary. Now, clients are much better informed about what they are looking for and are also alarmed at the prospect of encountering the coaching equivalent of the cowboy builder who charges a fortune for fixing the roof which never had anything wrong with it in the first place. Clients now routinely ask us what our quality control procedures are and what qualifications we and our associates hold. You must have robust answers to these questions. Training and accreditation will not guarantee that you get work but without it you will face unnecessary struggle.

This is a list of questions to ask yourself about any company whose training interests you:

Does the company coach as well as train? This is important because people who only teach coaching will slowly but surely lose their contact with the live issues that clients bring.

Are these coach trainers successful as coaches? Ask how long they have had full diaries and what level of clients they work with.

Ask for contacts with former participants so that you can get frank feedback on the quality of the training.

What is the learner–tutor ratio? Look for no more than 8:1. Some coach training courses are vast, with up to 100 people and one tutor. This means that lecturing is inevitably the main means of training with a focus on teaching rather than on learning.

How much of the course is face-to-face supervised practice? The sign of a poor course is one where the face-to-face content is limited. It's cheaper for the company to recommend dozens of books, to focus the course on distance learning materials or to run teleclasses. The student does all the work with minimal input from the tutors. This may make the course cheap to buy and profitable for the company running the training but may also mean that you get minimal feedback on your coaching. I strongly believe that this is the crucial lever in the fast growth of any individual's coaching skills.

Who is the accreditor? What status do they have? A university may be less impressive than it seems if it is one of the many former polytechnics still struggling to establish its academic credentials. If the providers accredit the course themselves, beware. There will be no external check on standards.

Is the accreditation linked to one of the main UK providers of such accreditation? We have thrown our lot in with the European Coaching and Mentoring Council (EMCC) and the Institute of Leadership and Management (ILM) but there are others.

How is the accreditation done? Be suspicious of anything where the emphasis is just on writing essays and learning sets. The heart of any good coach training should be on direct feedback on your coaching, ideally from recorded or observed sessions with actual clients, not just other course participants, robustly assessed with copious feedback from your tutor. This is expensive to provide, which is why so many coach training organizations do not provide it.

What claims does the company make about the attractiveness of coaching as a profession? Be suspicious of any that make it sound easy: it's not.

How are you treated when you call to enquire about the course? You may be relentlessly pursued by breathless offers from people impertinently over-using your first name, suggesting that if you buy now you can save 10 per cent. This offer, allegedly, will only last for the next few weeks. When this happens, you are in the grip of a sales organization not a training organization. My advice would be to look elsewhere.

Internal or external practice?

Most of this book assumes that you will be setting up as an independent executive coach. However, many organizations are investing in an internal coaching service because they have seen the value that their senior people obtain from working with external coaches. The argument goes like this: the most senior people will always prefer to have the apparent objectivity of the external coach, but when it is clear that coaching has been hugely valuable to these people, shouldn't we have this skilled help available for our middle managers? Answer: we should.

As an internally based coach, you have these advantages:

Easy access to your target population. This will include constantly meeting them informally as well as being able to access them through an intranet and email.

Unforced opportunities to do long-term follow-up work with clients.

Opportunities to observe your clients in action – an unrivalled source of feedback-gathering.

You will know who the gatekeepers and decision-makers are without anyone having to explain it.

You will cost less than your external rivals.

Ready understanding of the corporate culture and the context this creates for your clients – no one will need to explain the acronyms and jargon because you already know them; you will know what problems the culture may be creating for your clients.

Your disadvantages are:

You have a smaller pond to fish in – this may not matter if you are working in a large organization.

You have to live with your reputation – fine if it's high, not so good if you run into problems.

Sharing the same blind spots as your clients.

People may worry about confidentiality.

Hierarchy may make it more difficult for you to be taken seriously. People may also believe that the external coach has more glamour or can bring wider experience from other organizations.

In practice, virtually all of the principles recommended in this book will apply if you are running an internally based coaching service. You have to do high-quality work. You have to focus your offer, promote it and target your clients. You have to make the benefits of what you offer as tangible as possible. You have to compete for people's time and attention, and possibly compete with external coaches too. There will probably be an internal charge (*wooden pounds*) for what you do. The apparent differences are less important than you may think. In effect you will be running a business within a business – and with similar risks of failure and similar rewards for success.

How long does it take to build a coaching business?

It all depends – of course.

Here are some of the relevant factors. Fill in this questionnaire for yourself to estimate how long it could take for you.

	Agree		Disagree
I already have six current coaching clients	1	2	3
I hold a coaching qualification	1	2	3
I have specialist expertise relevant to the coaching I propose to do	1	2	3
I am credible to my potential clients	1	2	3
I network widely with people in other fields	1	2	3
I am continuing my professional development as a coach	1	2	3
I have other skills that could feed me coaching clients (e.g. facilitation, HR, training)	1	2	3
I am 100 per cent committed to establishing a career as a coach	1	2	3
I am organized and efficient	1	2	3
I am prepared to spend most of my first six months on marketing	1	2	3
I have a track record in successfully selling services	1	2	3
I see myself as an energetic entrepreneur	1	2	3
I can sustain myself financially while I am building my practice	1	2	3
I am currently operating in a field similar to coaching	1	2	3
Total points in each column			
OVERALL TOTAL			

Interpretation

Each point represents four potential weeks of effort before you are likely to be at take-off point with a coaching practice.

Assumptions

It's easier to establish a coaching practice with clients from an organization where you are already known and respected.

The nearer your current profession is to coaching, the easier it is likely to be to gain acceptance as a coach.

Coaching success is underpinned by aptitude, skill development, training and feedback, plus specialist interests.

To be a successful coach, you need entrepreneurial energy, selling skill and confidence in the likelihood of your own success.

Absolute essentials

- Accept the reality of the self-employed lifestyle: uncertainty and freedom go hand in hand.
- Be prepared to put time, money and energy into the process of developing the business, including into selling.
- Have a reliable way of supporting yourself financially while you are building the business.
- Choose or create a suitably neutral, friendly and business-like venue for your coaching.
- Invest in a decent computer with back-up for your files – and a separate telephone line if you are working from home.
- Get properly trained and accredited as a coach.

Undaunted? If yes, then the next stage is to do some hard thinking about what you offer your target market.

2 Positioning: Identifying Your Niche

This chapter is about how to identify the niches that will work for you. What do you want to offer to the coaching market? Where will you be credible? Where will you position yourself?

What is your offer to your market? The answer can't be *anything and everything*. If you look around the high street at firms in trouble, you will see that their failures invariably have to do with inability to answer that question clearly. A satisfying shopping trip will be one where you can answer these questions positively in relation to any shop you visit

Is there is a high chance that you will be able to buy the goods you want at a price you can afford?

Do you identify yourself strongly as one of their typical customers?

Is it equally obvious who is *not* their target customer?

So, for instance, your teenage son will scorn the chain of shops cunningly targeting his younger sister with attractive trinkets that can be bought for pocket money. You may not see the lure of the shop selling hundreds of apparently identical sports shoes that so fascinates the young males in your life.

A successful business is always clear about whom it does not want as a customer. For instance, for some businesses, conveying the exclusivity of wealth and privilege is at the core of their strategy and as long as there are enough rich people who actually want what they offer, they may well flourish. Similarly, there is no pop group in the world which appeals to everybody. In fact some of the most successful groups of all time – for instance the Rolling Stones – have positively gloried in alienating the people they most definitely did not want as fans. The best advice you could give any aspiring restaurateur would be to specialize in one or two *signature dishes*. This could be the lobster smoked over old whisky barrels cooked for a 'G8' summit meeting in a Scottish hotel or the superb, budget-priced home-made beefburger offered by a local high street restaurant. The way to fail is to have an enormous menu which can only be serviced by secret recourse to a large stock of ready-made frozen dishes delivered by a mass catering company.

Success as a coach is no different. It starts with hard thinking about what you are offering and to whom. You do not need or want *everybody* as your customer. Without the clarity that such thinking will provide, your enterprise will struggle.

You have to know what you want to work on with clients, which clients have these issues and – equally importantly – which clients will find you credible. This is the essence of *positioning*: deciding which market you are in and who your target client is. Another way of putting it is that you are identifying a niche. In fact most successful coaches will identify maybe three niche markets in which they can happily operate.

Your own expertise

It starts here. What are your particular areas of expertise and interest? Let's assume that you have coaching expertise, but that is not enough to target a market – it is a basic that all clients will hope to take for granted. You may believe that you have broad-based expertise – and indeed you might. But starting from the other end will probably gain you more clients: what do you have that most other coaches do not? This might be a clutch of related skills or one that leads to all the others. The questions that follow could help you to find the answers.

What specialized knowledge do you have?

Anything is possible here. Some examples of particular areas valuable to practising coaches in my own network have included:

job-hunting expertise gathered while working for an executive search company;

stress-management techniques learnt over a long career as a health professional;

close knowledge of the education world and the problems of senior leaders inside it, gathered through working first as Deputy Head of a secondary school and then as a local authority adviser;

selling-skills acquired from working in a business development role in a variety of big legal practices;

understanding the management, personal and spiritual issues involved for senior Church professionals as a result of a lifetime working in and around the Anglican Church;

presentation and voice skills learnt as an actor;

sound practical advice on debt management acquired while working as a personal finance adviser for an insurance company;

knowledge of managerial basics such as time management and delegation gained during an early career as a line manager and then as a management trainer;

personal experience of learning how to manage a stammer, making it possible to help other people with the same problem;

hypnosis: curiosity first piqued by being on the receiving end while giving up smoking, followed by undertaking a formal course;

weight loss and nutritional knowledge gathered from working for a specialist publisher;

tools and techniques for strategic thinking learnt while working in a large management consultancy.

What issues do you especially enjoy working on with clients?

When you have had some experience as a coach you will begin to notice that there are some topics which you relish. You find it fascinating to see how quickly clients can move when you are working together on these issues. These areas may be of long-standing interest to you or relatively recent – it doesn't matter. You will notice that both you and your client come alive when you are working in these areas. Such topics will have this flavour:

You feel confident because you are on home territory.

It is enjoyable to share your enthusiasm.

The feeling of satisfaction persists long after the client has left.

What are your talents?

The chances are that your areas of special interest will link closely with your unique talents and strengths. In Marcus Buckingham and Donald Clifton's interesting book, *Now Discover Your Strengths*, they work from the principle that being an all-round wonderful and competent human being is impossible. They offer the proposition that trying to address so-called *development needs* – a euphemism for weaknesses – is by and large a pointless exercise. Instead, they say that a better route is to acknowledge that each person has unique talents and that our greatest growth areas are in our strengths.

To identify your talents they suggest three initial questions – all of them thought-provoking and useful for any coach.

What *yearnings* did you have as a child? What were you constantly drawn to? The entrepreneur Richard Branson was successfully trading with other children before he was a teenager. The Bronte sisters created hand-written books as children, even though they only had each other as readers. A talent for acting or music usually shows itself early in a compulsion to perform or create. Some children show an early ability to lead and organize, to debate and persuade, to excel at sport or to solve scientific puzzles. Where were you aware that your interests were different from those of other children? When you identify these childhood passions they will have had the feeling of an itch that has to be scratched. What were yours?

Rapid learning: where did you outstrip your classmates? What has always been easy for you? Where are you puzzled when you look at the struggles of others and compare how simple it is for you? Which skills have you been able to acquire at speed, even if you have been introduced to them relatively late in your career?

Satisfaction: when do you experience that wonderful sensation of being *in flow* or as athletes say, *in the zone*? This is the point in the contest where the athletes know that they will win. There is a feeling of time passing quickly, of doing the thing you were born to do, of experiencing simultaneous relaxation and exhilaration and knowing that you can't wait to experience it all over again.

When you put these three sets of answers together, you will probably have a set of talents. To thrive as a coach, you need to embrace the talents that are unique for you. Jennifer Aston is one of the UK's top image consultants and coaches. She has appeared many times on television and in newspapers, has coached numerous people in the public eye and is a partner in the Image and Brand consultancy, Aston+Hayes (www.aston-hayes.com). She has the unusual skill of being able to deliver a tough message with kindness and tact. She experiences her work as fun and energizing. Her target clients are senior people in the public eye whose images are not well aligned to the impact they want and need to make, and who are open to change:

Jennifer Aston
Even as a 12-year-old I was confidently organizing fashion shows in my school, working with classmates on how they could dress well

for a disco, a school field trip or for church. I don't really know how I learnt my core skills, I always seem to have been able to do it and in fact both my mother and my grandmother are very smartly dressed women, so maybe it runs in the family. It's never occurred to me to doubt my judgement and even as a teenager I'd freely offer advice to my contemporaries – 'don't slouch', 'it would be better if you repaired that hem', and so on. After a first career as an editor, I was made redundant and decided to follow my true love – image consultancy – and quickly got myself qualified. It wasn't difficult to build my skills. My satisfaction is in seeing the immediate impact my advice can make for clients: I know they'll get more out of life.

In Jennifer's story you can see how clearly all three areas have come together. The attraction to colour and fashion, the yearning to improve image for others, the confidence in her own judgement, rapid learning of the craft, the talent for influencing and the deep satisfaction of being able to make immediate practical improvement in people's lives.

What is the equivalent for you?

What are clients willing to buy?

Clients do not typically wake up one morning and think, 'Oh it would be nice to find a coach today because I need to reach my true potential' or, 'I think I need to develop my inner resourcefulness.' They are no more than mildly interested in you or in the underlying philosophy of coaching. The trigger is some kind of problem. Most clients would probably prefer not to have a coach because they would rather not have the problem. Whereas you will try to position your offer as an investment, the client will see it as a cost. If it is a cost, then it has to have a benefit which justifies the money. With either executive or life coaching, the client only makes the purchase because they have probably already exhausted all the other options.

Change

The underlying motivator is always change. If nothing is changing in the client's life then it is unlikely he or she will need a coach.

In organizations, typical motivators would be:

Growing: expansion; making an acquisition; merging	Downsizing
Regulatory pressures	Competitor pressure
New senior management makes new demands	Technological change

All these changes will have impact on your potential clients, raising questions for them and the people who manage them:

My job could disappear: where would I go next?

I don't have all the skills I need for this work.

I can't get on with this new boss.

I don't have the team I need to do this work.

Similarly, in personal or life coaching, there needs to be a challenging set of changes: for instance, a milestone birthday, a new job, the loss or acquisition of a partner, health and fitness issues.

Whatever the context, there are certain clumps of topics that virtually all coaching can encompass:

Relationships:

Examples: better and more fulfilling relationships upwards, sideways or downwards in work contexts; with family members and friends; creating greater intimacy; finding a new partner.

Career:

Examples: how to decide on or change career; how to enter or exit a job; deciding whether or when to go into self-employment, retire or go part-time; starting and running a business.

Money:

Examples: how to get more of it or manage it better; managing a reduced budget, including how to manage debt.

Health: physical and mental.

Examples: how to reduce weight, get fitter, lead a healthier lifestyle; manage a chronic illness more effectively; how to reduce stress.

Leisure:

Examples: acquiring new skills to do with sport, fitness or hobbies; improving the home environment.

Work–life balance:

Examples: keeping the corporate pressures at bay if the organization is one where there is a long-hours culture; re-establishing the importance of leisure and family.

Leadership and job skills:

Examples: influencing; personal impact; communication; delegation; team development; managing time; prioritizing; decision-making; acquiring organizational savvy; strategic thinking.

Spirituality and personal growth:

Examples: finding greater happiness; finding new skills to learn; increasing peace of mind; increasing spiritual awareness; identifying overall life purpose.

All of these issues potentially create problems for which people are prepared to pay money to find answers. Many will be interlinked – for instance, a client with work–life balance problems will most probably also have issues over time-management and prioritization. The question is: which of them contains the possible target market for you because they are areas in which you already have expertise?

Credibility with clients

You may feel you have an impressive track record in your chosen area, but will it impress clients? In most areas of coaching, clients want proof that you understand their world.

Formal qualifications

If you share a common vocational qualification, then you are immediately over one possible hurdle. So, for instance, Dr Susan Kersley (www.thedoctorscoach.co.uk) is now a professional coach specializing in coaching other doctors. She has no need to prove that she understands how medicine can seem like a way of life rather than just a job, or how stressful the role is, because she has been there herself. Her doctor clients do not need to spend time spelling out their clinical and ethical dilemmas because she already understands the jargon and the context.

At the same time, you need to regard these possible entry-points as merely opening doors. As one coach tartly remarked to me about his attempts to gain a foothold in the world of banking, *All senior bankers want a 40-year-old coach just like themselves with all the same qualifications and background, but then they are going to ask, why isn't he still in banking if he's that good?* Having left your clients' world long enough ago to make it clear that you are not competing with them is probably your best bet here. Even better may be some track record of working in their industry without actually having worked in their functional area, for instance working in a pharmaceutical company without having been a scientist, or working at a newspaper without ever having been a journalist.

You may hold other qualifications – for instance a Master's degree in occupational psychology, or be a member of a professional institute such as those for people in marketing or engineering. Any of these could increase your acceptability to clients in similar fields. Be aware that some professional areas are highly qualification-conscious: you will spot them from the way clients habitually add letters after their names. Even if you could not be expected to have a matching qualification, clients may still expect you to display equivalent academically verified expertise.

Just occasionally you might want to down-play a qualification. For instance, holding a psychotherapeutic qualification may deter the more naïve organizational client who holds irrational prejudices about therapy.

Your industry or sector experience

Clients like to work with people who are recognizably like them. It is always easier to sell successfully when this is the case. When you share a professional background with people, the chances are that you will have other common interests. The industry or sector where you have most recently worked will also be where you have most of your contacts. Unless you have good reasons for leaving this sector behind, such as finding its typical people unbearable, it will be madness to ignore the advantages these contacts give you. Where you already know people in your target market it is going to be much easier to gain access. This will facilitate introductions, enable you to demonstrate your familiarity with the organization and its culture, or, if you are doing life-coaching, to show that you understand the social networks of your target clients. Clients will also be able quietly to check you out with colleagues or friends rather than just relying on their own first impressions.

Experience in itself is never enough. What is your actual reputation in your field? Some beginner coaches are unaware that their self-perception is significantly adrift from how their target market sees them. There are two common problems here. One especially applies to people whose departure from their previous employer has been acrimonious. Where the underlying reason for this is poor performance, such people may be deluding themselves if they believe that everyone shares their own high opinion of their abilities. Word will already have circulated that the reason for the departure was mediocrity or failure. This will make immediate success as a coach in that sector unlikely. If you have the slightest of doubts here, get your courage up and ask at least three trusted friends to answer this question:

What's my reputation in the industry/firm/sector?

Coaches may claim, rightly or wrongly, that it does not matter whether you have sector experience or not, but the point is that clients almost always think it matters. An example in practice of how this is applied was a so-called Coaching Fair for senior police officers. This grisly event was part of a course where the officers were told that choosing a coach was a mandatory part of the programme: in itself a clumsy and wrong-footing beginning to the relationship. Seven coaching companies had stalls around the conference centre where the course was taking place. Each officer was equipped with a list of six questions, in effect criteria for making the choice, the first of which was, *How many other senior police officers have you coached?* However excellent the coach, those whose answer was 'none' or 'two or three' left without clients. The company that came away with the majority of the work had been working with uniformed services for many years and its managing director was a non-executive member on the Board of the training organization delivering the programme. This was possibly a position that risked accusations of conflict of interest, but it was certainly working as a guarantee that they understood their clients' world.

Most clients expect you to know something of the industry in which they operate. Being able to make unforced references to the overall issues and challenges, to ask well-informed questions, to use the jargon artlessly – all of this will increase your credibility. This is hard to do without at least some hands-on experience of working with the people in the organization.

Even if clients know that it could be unreasonable to expect detailed sector experience, they will want the reassurance of knowing that you have already worked with people whose responsibilities are recognizably in the same genre as their own. For instance, in talking to several recently appointed ambassadors looking for a coach, courtesy of a new scheme at the Foreign and Commonwealth Office, almost all asked me how many other senior clients I had worked with in similar roles. They named problems such as working through complex dilemmas posed by local and international politics, the loneliness and vulnerability sometimes associated with a foreign posting or the tangled issues involved in running a team of mixed British and locally appointed staff. It was important to my credibility with these interesting and talented people to be able to say that the answer was yes – I had never worked previously with an ambassador as such, but I had indeed worked with people in similarly demanding overseas roles.

Your age

If you want to coach people on their retirement plans, you will need to be within hailing distance of that age yourself to be credible. Similarly, few senior executives will want to be coached by someone half their age. If you are interested in the young graduate market, then you will be more acceptable to your potential clients and the parents who are probably paying the bill if you are still young enough not to look hopelessly past-it to the actual client but old enough to have the gravitas which will appeal to their parents.

Maturity and modelling

It should go without saying, but it is worth a reminder. You will need to be a model yourself in whatever field you are coaching. If you are coaching parents, then you need to be an exemplary parent yourself. When you work as a personal fitness coach you must look and be fit yourself. If you are working on managing stress or weight-control, you need to have your own stress under control and to be the correct weight for your height. Where you are doing career coaching you need to be able to demonstrate successful management of your own career.

Try working out the answers to these questions to see what emerges about what you want to offer to your market

My expertise	My passions, enthusiasms and talents	My track record and credibility
Spirituality /Christian	Grow in spiritual life Past are work	✓
Career /Holistic	people are in right career - 70% fit.	✓

People who have issues relevant to my expertise, talents and track record are
Their likely triggers for coaching will be

Narrowing the search through segmentation

You can learn a lot from looking at how large companies target their markets.

Many years ago, the Swiss watch industry revitalized itself when it realized that customers did not simply set out on a vague search to buy a watch. There was the customer who still wanted the classy Swiss timepiece which could become an heirloom, the customer who wanted a fun fashion item (hence the birth of Swatch), the customer who wanted a piece of jewellery and the one who wanted a cheap throw-away item which could be purchased from the local garage. These were very different market segments wanting very different products and needed to be reached in different ways.

You will also need to segment your market. Which of these categories might be relevant to your offer and help you refine your identikit portrait of your target client?

Possible factor in segmenting	Relevance to your offer
Geography: region; city, town?	
Sector or industry?	
Size of organization?	
Typical organizational challenges?	
Typical age of client?	
Profession?	
Seniority?	
Personal circumstances?	
Job role?	
Gender?	
Ethnic group?	
Income?	
Familiarity of this market with coaching?	
Size of this market?	
Other?	

Size

The size of your target markets may be particularly important in coaching. In other professional service areas, once a client is secured, inertia or continuing demands may sustain the relationship. For instance, in accountancy, all limited companies must have annually audited accounts. This is not true of coaching. The relationships are short, so the client pipeline needs to be constantly refreshed. If you want to work full-time in coaching, you will need to secure four or five new clients every month. This implies not only continuing marketing effort on your part but also a market that is actually big enough for you to be able to find that number of clients, possibly in sharp competition with other coaches. Where you are offering life coaching, US experience seems to show that it is only the most affluent who buy, so you need to have enough well-off people in your target population to make your business viable.

In the end it comes down to a number of overlapping questions:

- What are you really passionate about and want to offer your target market?
- What are you qualified to offer?
- Who is your typical client?
- Which problems can you work on with these clients?
- How do your target clients describe their problems?
- When you look at your target market from the perspective of the potential client, what credibility do you have?
- Which market segments can you identify as a good match for what you are offering?
- Are these segments big enough to sustain a coaching practice?

I strongly advise you to use this list to write a profile of your target client or clients. It will help you get clear about who you are aiming at and why. Here is how two other coaches did it:

> *Vincent (a freelance management development trainer)*
> It was so frustrating to see people on my courses and to know how much more learning they could do one-to-one. I was well liked in the company and when they announced they were doing a huge staff reduction exercise I realized I was soundly positioned to launch my coaching offer.
>
> My target clients were the youngish high fliers based in the HQ building. They had been taken on in the expectation of a fast-track technological-cum-managerial career and were now going to be made redundant. I saw their problems as being: how to recover confidence; how to identify what they really wanted from a new job; how to write a snazzy CV which gave proper focus to their skills; how to present themselves for interview and then how to manage their exits gracefully. I have specialist knowledge of all of these topics.
>
> I knew that I had a far greater and more detailed understanding of all this than my competitors. I approached my potential

commissioning contacts with a highly specific offer. This really paid off and I was working with anything from five to seven of my target cohort at any one time over the next year. As my clients did get new jobs, I knew that they would probably take me with them into their new companies, and this is exactly what has happened.

Edith

It was proving difficult to maintain my job as Human Resources Director with my commitments as a wife and mother. With three small children and a husband in a demanding job, I was always exhausted. I retrained as a coach, knowing that this was something I had always wanted to do and felt I was good at. HR as a profession has always fascinated me – it can potentially do so much and yet so many HR departments are reviled. I did HR interim management while I was building my coaching practice. This took nearly two years before it was self-sustaining. My initial target clients were the most senior HR professionals already likely to know what coaching could do and to be in a position to control their own budgets. This meant they probably worked for organizations with at least 5000 employees, or else worked in a knowledge-worker organization with a turnover above a certain level. I assumed a geographical base of Greater London because I wanted to reduce the amount of travel I did and I thought that area was big enough to give me plenty of scope.

I didn't segment by sector, but in fact all my early clients were from the retail sector, which is where all my best contacts were. I knew that what they would say to themselves about their problems was stuff like

No one takes me as seriously as I take myself.

My HR team is demoralized and exhausted.

I can't be operational and strategic all at the same time but that's what the organization seems to want from me.

My Chief Executive wants quick fixes but I know they don't work.

Who can I talk to who will understand this and help me to find a way through it?

Everything I said and wrote about my offer showed that I could work with clients to find answers to these questions. If I did good work with them, I also knew that they were going to be able to recommend me to my next target: specialist professionals in their first senior leadership roles.

Most coaches have two or three niches. They might be closely related or distinctly different.

Fees

The question every new coach wants to have answered is *What should I charge?* Approach the answer to this question by answering another set of questions.

1 What do you need to earn?

Make a list of all your actual outgoings: energy bills, rent or mortgage, food, gifts, holidays, clothes, car, telephony, subscriptions, training ... Decide how many days in the year you aim to be doing billable work: the usual number for a full-time job would be 150. Divide your outgoings total by the number of days to see how much your rock bottom target fee per day should be, then divide by the number of hours you want to deliver coaching on any given day. Six hours is the maximum that most coaches can deliver and stay sane. Since the outgoings total usually comes to a much smaller sum than any of us imagines, this hourly rate is likely to be modest: it represents the bottom-line cost of putting yourself on the market.

Another way of doing the same calculation is to start with the salary you earned in your last (or current) job, remembering to double it to include the actual cost of employing you – overheads, insurance, PA support and so on. Divide again by the number of working days you propose, then divide again to get to an hourly fee.

However, being paid on the basis of what you need has never been the way the world rewards its workers, but this may be a sum that can form the foundation of further thinking, not least as a motivator.

2 How do you want to sell coaching and bill clients?

There are a number of different ways that this can be done. In the US, the usual method is to bill by the month, with an agreed number of thirty-minute or one-hour phone-based sessions assumed to fall within that time. This is much less common in the UK. There are two alternatives: charging by the hour or session and charging for an entire coaching programme. I greatly prefer to charge for a whole programme, making a rapid estimate before the coaching starts of what the client is likely to need. Brief coaching – for instance, a single session – is deeply unsatisfying because it is inevitably superficial.

Another variant of the whole-programme approach is to offer unlimited access to the coach for a set period of time. I do offer this as a possibility, but warily. The reason is an ethical one. The overall price for an entire year of access to you and to any other specialist coaches in your network on demand can seem like a lot of money and both you and your client have to know that the client really will take full advantage of it. The busier and more senior the client, the less likely it is that they will feel able to make frequent spaces for you in their diaries. I once acted as supervisor to a fellow coach from a firm where this was the only way they sold their services. In his sessions we returned again and again to his unease about the fact that so few of his clients ever took up their full entitlement. One of my own former clients returned to me for some top-up coaching after a spell with a coach from another company where this was also the practice. Here the discomfiture was with the client: *My coach seemed more needy of me than I was of him* she told me wryly, *He was constantly on the phone trying to fix up sessions.* I privately interpreted this as guilt that his company was taking money for services that it was not actually delivering. If this method of billing attracts you, there is an alternative to asking for the whole year's work as an up-front payment (the norm for this kind of contract). This is to bill quarterly or half-yearly on the basis of a review with clients about the value they are getting from the work, offering the option of ending at that point.

It is always more difficult to negotiate extra sessions later. Clients may feel diffident about asking their funders for more. Life-coaching clients may have to square the additional expense with partners and may hesitate for the same reasons. A whole-project approach always seems better. I make it clear to clients that the face-to-face part of the coaching is just the front end of the process. They are free to email me or consult me by telephone (short conversations assumed) between sessions – for instance to report on how they have got on with their 'homework' or to tell me how a particularly tricky meeting, discussed and planned-for at our session, has gone. On the relatively rare occasions where the coaching is finished more quickly than anticipated, we will offer a refund, or, in the case of organizational buyers, a credit for another client.

I notice that beginner coaches are often too diffident in what they suggest here. In their hearts they know that the client is likely to need six two-hour sessions, not three, yet they pitch for three out of timidity.

There is a link here with the venue that you choose for coaching. When clients are coming to you, as ours virtually always do, this makes two-hour sessions seem like better value for the investment in travel time that the client is making. Similarly, a busy client and a busy coach will usually need at least three weeks between sessions to find slots when both are available. Telephone-based coaching is almost always based on one-hour slots and may happen more frequently, perhaps weekly.

3 Competitor pricing

Look at the coaches whose experience is most like yours and who are providing services which most resemble your own and to similar clients. What are they charging? This will give you clues about your own fee levels.

4 Geography

Your geographical area will have a bearing on fees. Where costs of living are low, fee levels will also be low. Similarly, UK prices are often a great deal higher than prices in the rest of Europe or the US because our cost of living is so much higher.

5 The salary of your target client

This is a strange phenomenon but your own fee level should roughly equate with the earnings of your target client. This is why the few coaching companies working exclusively with FTSE 100 Chairs and Chief Executives can ask the extremely high fees that they do. Roughly speaking, the more senior the potential client, the more of a premium rate the buyer will expect to pay and vice versa. In making the calculation, do the same sum that you did on your own needs and former salary. It does actually cost at least twice gross salary to employ someone and few people are productive for more than 150 days in the year so when you know their salary, it is actually easy to work out what hourly rate your client is earning.

Be alert to the fact that the market will resist paying the same rate for coaching a junior manager as for coaching the Chief Executive in the same organization. This is why it is important not to confuse your market by offering the same service to both.

Another possibility in executive coaching is to set up a yearly unlimited access contract on the basis of a percentage of the client's gross salary. I have always been uncomfortable with this principle and have never been tempted to use it, though I know some coaches who believe that it is fair.

6 Years of experience

The market rewards successful experience and this is as true of coaching as it is elsewhere. By successful experience, I mean successful experience as a coach, not in your previous career. When you can point to track record as evidence of why a client should hire you, that is one of the markers for fixing your fee. Roughly speaking, you can add 10 per cent to your fee for every year of success as a coach. So if you start with the lowest base-line rate for whichever branch of coaching you plan to operate in, you should be able to charge 10 per cent more for each additional year. This is why coaches who have proved that they can thrive for eight years will be charging double the rates asked for by a beginner and those with twelve years or more of successful practice can ask three times the beginner rate.

7 Sector rates

There are differences between sectors and what they expect to pay. So for instance, the voluntary sector is always acutely aware that they must manage their administrative costs and will be challenged if they don't. If they are part of your target market, depending on the nature of their funding, they may expect to pay less than clients in the public sector. Similarly, public sector clients may expect lower fees than their counterparts in FTSE 500 companies. FTSE 100 companies may be affronted if they are *not* charged large fees. These are generalizations. Individual clients may buck the trends.

8 What the market will pay

In the end your true fee level is what your chosen market will pay for your services and this will be determined by how they rate you as much as by what they are paying your competitors. On the celeb circuit, the A-list can command what can seem like ridiculous prices for a single after-dinner speech. Are they really worth it? Maybe not, but if that is what the buyer will pay, then the answer is yes, it's a market like anything else.

So as with any other market, the coaching market will pay for glamour and scarcity value. If your market knows that you have coached government ministers or famous actors, then it may assume that some of this apparent glamour will rub off on them. Some clients like to boast about *My coach X who has also been coach to famous person Y.*

Remember here that you do not need everyone as your client. You will be too cheap for some clients and too dear for others. This does not matter as long as there are enough potential clients in your target market.

Price resistance

Clients may tell you that you are too expensive. The reason is always that they do not rate you at your own valuation. This may have a number of underlying causes

> They are inexperienced buyers. This may apply in either the corporate or the life-coaching arena. For instance, a potential client for life coaching may not be used to paying professional fees of any sort. If this characterizes your target market then you are probably aiming at the wrong niche.

They are buying on price, not on value.

They are equating your service with another service which has lower prices. For instance, a buyer who believes that coaching is just another form of training will expect to pay an appropriate slice of a day's training fee. You may equate coaching much more with consulting – normally rewarded at a significantly higher rate than training. In the life-coaching arena, clients may expect to pay therapy rates for coaching. In general, these are lower than fees for coaching.

They expect you to be flattered by the chance to work for them. A client of my own reliably informs me from direct experience that some members of the royal family act on this principle and we have encountered it ourselves with certain household-name client organizations.

It is a buyer's market and the buyer believes that he or she can drive prices down on the assumption, possibly mistaken, that there are plenty of other people who can do just as good a job.

They are working in a sector which is strapped for cash or which resists the apparent indulgence of coaching (the voluntary sector is an example).

You have failed to differentiate yourself or to sell the benefits of what you offer.

Only you can assess which of these – or more than likely a combination of them – is operating in your own case when you encounter them. You have three choices. You can bite back your disappointment, agree to do the work at the lower rate and use it as an opportunity to assess whether this feedback is telling you something significant about your market value or whether it is just a one-off. You can haggle in the hope of reaching a compromise figure. Or you can walk away from the work.

Starting too low

It is easy to start too low. Early on in my coaching career I went to pitch for some work at what was then the accountancy company, Price Waterhouse. I was receiving a warm reception from the 'gatekeeper' client until the moment when I was asked about fees. I interpreted the look of horror on my would-have-been buyer's face as resistance to what I thought was the high level of fee I named. In fact she gently informed me that I was too cheap to coach the partners she had in mind. *They will only work with people charging at much the same level they charge for their own time and that's double your rate.* We parted on good terms but I never had work from this client, although I now regularly coach partners in other big financial services consultancies, having learnt my lesson.

If you do start too low: beware. It will be difficult to raise your fees with those clients later and you may find yourself pegging fees at an unrealistically low level for some years after you have raised them with newer clients. If you think that your fees are too low for your level of expertise, you will feel resentful: not a good state for a coach. When you find yourself overwhelmed with requests for coaching, that could be a sign that your fees are too low. You can sometimes reduce the demand by raising the price, although it may surprise you to discover that clients care less about the price than you think.

Differential pricing

You need to have a policy on where and how you will discount fees. It may send an uncomfortable message to your market if, for instance, you are offering exactly the same service to individuals as to corporate clients but at half the fee. The discomfort is that the service is identical so the corporate client may end up feeling like a mug and resentful at having to subsidize other people, while the individual client could still feel that the cost is far too high. You could also end up with a situation where you are competing with yourself – for instance offering perverse incentives for clients to buy at lower rates. In the end the answer to this question comes down to which niche you are aiming for. I will normally pass on requests from individuals paying for themselves to other trusted coaches who operate in this market at lower rates.

We will always negotiate over fees, as long as these conditions are met:

We have spare capacity and it is better to get some work than none. If the requested coach has a full diary then there is no incentive to reduce rates.

Our brand will not be damaged by agreeing to or suggesting a lower rate.

Market conditions favour the buyer.

The buyer is prepared to accept a slightly less experienced coach for the sake of saving on his or her budget.

The work is interesting and would give us valuable experience of a new market that we wish to enter – or to assess in order to decide whether we want to enter it or not.

The client is a worthy cause to which we wish to contribute. In this case we will always make the nature of the discount clear on the invoice so that the client understands the market value of the gift. In general we follow this particular principle only rarely as we have one charity (*Alone in London*) which we support generously with both money and services and this feels like a big enough contribution on the charitable front.

The client is offering guaranteed volume and is right to expect a discount on this basis.

Competitive advantage

Every business has competitors. In fact, if you have no competitors, it is dubious whether you have a viable business. You need to think hard about your competitive advantage. This useful concept means knowing where you differentiate yourself by adding value to clients, for instance through offering lower prices or through providing the superior service that justifies a higher price.

Competitive advantage means giving potential clients clear reasons for choosing you over competitors. You must have some products, services or resource that match a key buying criterion for your clients. It is about uniqueness. The real prize in any business is *sustainable competitive advantage*. This means an advantage that is sustainable as long as it continues to be perceived as valuable by customers and competitors cannot easily find a way to duplicate it.

The most useful sources of sustainable competitive advantage in the coaching market are the intangible ones. Examples might be the intellectual or psychological depth you could bring to coaching questions, the length of your experience as a coach or the detailed knowledge you possess of a client's business and problems, their needs, tastes and preferences and the long-term, mutually trustful nature of your relationship with them.

Research other coaches operating in the area you have chosen. This is easy to do: look at their websites and send for their brochures, if they have them. Try ringing them to enquire about their services and assess the quality of the responses you get. What do they say about themselves? What do they charge? Who are their clients? Why are those clients buying from them? There will be no single answer to these questions, rather it will be a blend of reasons. Here are two successful coaches talking about the competitive advantage of their offers. Both are women of similar age working in the area of executive coaching in the public sector and have selection-coaching as one of their offers, but in every other way they could not be more different:

> *Tilly*
> My target market is the higher reaches of government, including politicians, an area I know well because I worked in the Civil Service for many years. I also worked for an Executive Search firm before that. My speciality is people who are either entering or leaving their jobs, so the run-up to general elections and their aftermath is always a busy time for me. I can also back up any of my assertions with

3   Promoting Your Offer: Foundations

We coaches would love to believe that just doing wonderful coaching will generate new clients. Word of mouth is certainly a powerful recommendation, but it is unlikely that of itself it will ever generate enough clients to keep your business going. This is because:

Your current clients may speak warmly about you. But few of the people to whom they speak are likely to need coaching instantly.

Coaching is a short-term engagement, unlike, for instance, some types of therapy, so you need many clients in your sales pipeline (see also page 33).

Clients move on, retire or die, and successors will want to distance themselves from their predecessors' choices. This may be disappointing, but wishing to start on your own terms is human nature.

The organizations and social groups in which you are comfortable and welcomed will change – sometimes rapidly and out of all recognition. This could mean that your coaching offer is no longer a good match to what they need.

You have many competitors, and the sensible ones will be actively promoting their services.

So your business is unlikely to promote itself. This chapter looks at foundation promotional materials. In themselves they are unlikely to bring you clients, but you will need at least some of them to support you in the more active marketing activities described in the next chapter.

How you describe yourself

Benefits, not features or processes

Too many coaches believe that what they are selling is coaching. When they describe what they do, they talk proudly about the tools and techniques that they use such as Neuro-Linguistic Programming (NLP) or psychometric instruments. They use coaching jargon which should really only be exchanged in the privacy of a room containing other coaches. This is why so many coaching brochures read as if they have been written by the same person – someone who has just left a coach-training programme on a surge of enthusiasm. Think for a moment about your contact with other professionals. If you need a hip replacement, do you really want to know what instruments the surgeon will be using? If you were briefing an architect, would you be interested in hearing about the particular kind of computer program she proposed to employ to draw up your plans? If you are hiring a plumber, do you want him to show you the rods and spanners that he uses? Of course not. You are only interested in getting your hip working again, your house well designed or your plumbing issue sorted.

Clients only want to know what problems you can solve for them. Any curiosity they have about the actual coaching process will be quickly sated. How you get there is far less significant than the promise that you will produce results.

The best salespeople know how to emphasize the benefits of the product or service, not its features. This is the distinction:

A *feature* is a relatively neutral descriptive phrase. It describes characteristics: size, length of time, colour, age, technical data, price, methodology or process. Features have little persuasive power.

A *benefit* is what added value the feature brings and identifies what need the potential purchaser will satisfy through buying. For instance, if you are buying a car, compare the relative power of these phrases:

Feature	Benefit
0 – 50 in × seconds	Rapid acceleration gets you out of trouble quickly in an emergency
Leather seats	Leather upholstery is cool in summer and warm in winter; wears beautifully
Satellite navigation pack included in every car	Wherever you are, you will never get lost
ABS keeps base brakes from locking up, automatically pumping the braking system	These brakes ensure that you maximize the chances of braking safely, even on wet or slippery roads

As coaches we should not confuse features with benefits when writing or speaking about our services, yet many of us do. We talk about our own backgrounds, our methods, techniques and processes and list all the services we can provide, as if they are ends in themselves; then we expect clients to work out the connections with the results they will get from the coaching.

Compare these two descriptions:

> XXX Coaching is one of London's premier coaching companies. All three partners, X, Y and Z, are trained in Neuro-Linguistic Programming (NLP) and hold Master Practitioner Certificates. All three also hold MBAs. Together they have 10 years of coaching experience, after distinguished earlier careers in A, B and C industries. Their focus is on senior leaders. The company offers leadership coaching, leadership development training, facilitation, organization development services, seminars, and training for other coaches.

This copy is unlikely to generate interest among target clients. It is a list of features, with no benefits. It is about selling, not buying. It focuses on the partners – but not in a way that is likely to intrigue a potential buyer. It lists a process (NLP) only likely to be understood by a minority, and ends with a list of services that is far too wide to be compelling. There is nothing in it to suggest a focused target client group or what results such clients might obtain from the coaching. After finding that this piece of copy did not do the trick, XXX Coaching might reframe the way they write about their offer:

> If you are a senior leader in the NHS, XXX Coaching can help. We understand the relentless pressure that government targets place on you – and the difficulty of squaring financial stringency with high-quality clinical services. We have many years of success in working with Chief Executives and Directors to maximize their talents, to develop their organizations and still have a satisfying private life. Ring us today on <> to discuss how we could help you through coaching.

This second attempt is much better. It is clear about the target – and, if they wish, the partners can produce alternative copy for the other markets in which they operate. It assumes a successful track record without forcing the qualifications of the partners on readers and it talks specifically about the benefits that will result from the coaching, ending with an invitation to action. Whatever you write about your offer, it should have these same characteristics:

- Clearly identify the target client.
- Focus on their problems.
- Identify the benefits and solutions your coaching will offer.
- End with a call to action.

These principles apply wherever you write or speak about your offer, whether it is in person, on the telephone, in a brochure or on a website.

Your company name

When you choose a child's name, you are making a powerful statement about yourself and your hopes for the child. Giving a child an apparently old-fashioned name could mean that either you are ahead of the pack or that you are tragically out of touch. Some names betray a person's probable age, and instantly identify their social and racial origins. It is the same with a company. You cannot avoid conveying an impression through the name you give it.

The place to start is with your target clients. What image do you need to convey to them? What will they find attractive? This is always a case for brainstorming: writing down, preferably with a friend, associate or partner, any word that comes to mind without prejudging or evaluating. Alternatively, use a thesaurus to spark your thinking. Look for at least thirty words. The most powerful words are verbs containing some link with change and the future. Examples might be:

Create	Produce	Transform
Change	Fast-track	Develop
Perform	Grow	Lead

You might then want to make a comparable list of nouns which identify the market in which you want to work. Other possibilities are a geographical association. Beware of making this too limiting. You may want to expand beyond the area implied by the name. Sometimes this may not be a narrowing factor – for instance with a town or city that has the right sort of associations. All those many private colleges aiming to teach foreigners English and which include the words *Oxford*, *London* or *Cambridge* in their names are explicitly trading on what they believe to be the high-status associations of these places.

Other words with powerful associations link with the benefits of the changes your coaching will produce:

Results	Solutions	Answers
Returns	Investments	Profit
Positives	Promise	Growth
Development	Learning	Achievement

Now highlight the ten or so words that seem most attractive to you. What combinations might create an interesting name for your company?

Should you use your own name? Probably not. First, it can convey either swaggering egotism or else plain lack of imagination. It also suggests a corner-shop approach. Initials, first names, jokes and winsome alliterations are no better. They will remind your clients of those small local companies who call their businesses *AD Builders*, *Hair Today* or *Tony's Trattoria*. If and when you expand your company, your colleagues may not be at all happy about a company that bears your name and it may also imply that you are the only principal in it – and by then that might not be the case. There are commercial exceptions to this – for instance, Marks & Spencer. But note that it's Apple Computer Inc., not Steve Jobs Computing Inc., The Body Shop International plc and not Anita's Cosmetics, and News Corp, not Murdoch Family Communications.

Exceptions

There is a modest case to be made for using your own name. When you have a considerable reputation in your target market, you might reasonably feel that you could capitalize on it. Some coaches also like the personal and intimate tone this conveys. As one such coach said to me, *I am actually what I am selling, so why wouldn't I use my name for my business?* This goes along with a parallel feeling that there is something unpretentious and authentic about making it clear that you are a solo operator. Commercially there may also be advantages as clients know they are going to get you as their coach and not, as they might fear, an inferior substitute.

Once you have got a combination of words that you like, test it further:

- Try it out on people who are good enough friends to be candid, and listen to what they say.
- Try it out on some sample clients. *New Age Coaching* may be just right for the alternative and holistic flavour of a coaching practice aimed at people who want to downshift to the good life, but will for certain be wrong if you want to attract tough MDs in manufacturing. It may also date you, in the same way that an *Ethel* told the world through her name that she was born in the early years of the twentieth century.
- Can you hear a PA say the name while answering the phone without squirming?
- Does it clearly state what market you are in?
- Does it sound unique – in other words avoiding sounding just like every other small coaching practice?
- Does it avoid stating the obvious? Many small companies fall into the trap of using platitudinous words like *professional*. Of course you are professional – that is the bare minimum, so claiming it in your title may leave the listener or reader with a so-what response.

You will need to check the name out – your accountant will be able to do this for you, or there are many websites that offer the same service. The flash of genius that has just given you the perfect name may already have been taken – or be too similar to another company's name for acceptability and may expose you to the charge of *passing off*. Some words are regarded as *sensitive* and their use is restricted – for instance, *Authority, International, Group, British* – and many more. For a quick guide to the rules, and how to take it further, visit www.businesslink.gov.uk

Your CV

I use the phrase *CV* with reluctance. *Brief biography* is a better term. What I am talking about is not the conventional two- to three-page career summary with your date of birth, whether or not you have a full driving licence and which university you attended, a full list of every employer, ending with your quirky hobbies and the amusing names of your cats. In 16 years as a coach, I have never yet sent or been asked for one of these documents and nor have any of my colleagues. However, you will often be asked by prospective clients to *send a CV*. What they mean is that they want a brief description of how you see yourself and why they should hire you – in other words, some advertising copy. You will want to include the same material on your website. Here is how to do it:

Paragraph 1	A general introduction saying succinctly what benefits you bring to which clients, written in the third person
Paragraph 2	Fleshes out paragraph 1 by giving details of clients you have worked with, the typical problems you work on with such clients and the kinds of results you get
Paragraph 3	Up to you: anything which distinguishes you from the herd. This could include adding some intriguing details about your earlier career, prizes you have won, relevant qualifications, books, articles, community responsibilities, your personal life, leisure pursuits

The format can vary, of course, depending on you and the audience you envisage reading the copy. Here is how our Associate, John Forrest, (www.johnforrest.tv) appears currently on our website:

John Forrest
John's coaching clients are senior business executives who need to know how to appear in front of the microphone and camera with confidence. He also specializes in coaching people to deal with the

media during a crisis – either for them or for their organization. John's unique approach enables his clients to stay in control, remain calm, be themselves and deliver a clear, positive message.

As a coach and consultant, John has worked with senior doctors, Chief Executives, Directors and others in a wide variety of sectors, including the NHS, the BBC, the Telegraph Group and the Labour Party. In more than 30 years, John's career has taken him around most sectors of the radio and TV industry as a producer. During his time as a BBC staff member he was involved in facilitating high-level advice groups on programme genres for the BBC's Board of Governors. He conducted various training workshops and several motivational events for staff members of SVT (Swedish Television). As well as coaching people to appear in front of the camera, he continues to train and mentor professionals in the broadcast industry and works as a broadcast consultant to several publishers and charities.

John's broadcast programmes have variously won nominations for acclaimed industry awards, including BAFTA, the Royal Television Society and he won a Sony Award for creative use of radio. As his training and coaching work continues to expand he also maintains his role in programme production for broadcast and corporate clients, thus ensuring that clients get the benefit of up-to-date input from a working producer.

Visual identity

You will need a visual identity for your business – a set of graphic images which will work smoothly across your stationery and electronic communications. It needs to work equally well on business cards, compliment slips, invoices, brochures, flyers, and all other materials you eventually produce, including handouts, tapes or books and your website.

The choice can seem impossibly wide, so some useful guidelines to start you thinking are:

- Go back to the work you have already done on your target market. What do you need to convey about yourself that would appeal to them?
- Scrutinize a batch of newspapers and magazines. Cut out any advertisements and logos that appeal. What is it about them that you like? Keep these for briefing your designer later.
- Avoid all those tempting symbols which have become graphic clichés: globes, light bulbs, ticks, arrows, acorns, apples, trees, balloons, clouds, sun, moon, stars, stick-people, compasses, rainbows, hearts,

flowers, doves, swallows, owls, handshakes – and that list is just for starters. Unless your designer is a genius, it's all been done before and better. I have a strong personal preference for simple logos that use typeface and company name – they look more elegant and do the job more effectively than any fancy stuff with tired symbols. Think British Airways, *The Economist* and Virgin – here the brand names are used as the logo and are instantly recognizable through their clean, distinctive typeface and style.

- Avoid using your photograph in a prominent position on any of your materials and especially avoid it on your business card. It looks naïve and puppyish – not the kind of impression you will want to make on your prospective clients.
- Keep it uncomplicated. Whatever your first attempt, ask yourself, *how could this be simplified?* Knowing when to stop elaborating is often the difference between good-enough and outstanding.
- Two colours rather than four will save you a lot of money at the printing stage. Your logo should work as well in black and white as it does in colour, since your material may be faxed or photocopied. For the same reason avoid colours which are too pale to photocopy clearly.

Working with designers

Unless you are a graphic designer yourself, this is not the time to indulge your inner artist. Go to a professional.

When choosing designers ask to see their portfolio and trust your own reactions. Look for confidence and stylishness. Assess what it would be like to work with them and ask for examples of how they have worked successfully with clients of all sorts. Someone may be a brilliant designer, but inflexible and tantrum-prone as a colleague. Ideally you want someone who will listen carefully and respectfully to your brief but who will also help you understand what can and can't be done through design, challenging you where necessary. Ask for and follow up references from other clients.

Give the designer your collection of cuttings and talk through why you like them. Assume that you will go through several iterations before you reach a design package that satisfies you. Show the final draft version to at least 10 people and ask for candid feedback. The best question is, *I'm thinking of using this as my company logo. I want honest feedback. What does it immediately suggest to you?* Just asking this question and choking back defensive ripostes may well save you from expensive disasters.

Once you have the absolutely final version, ask the designer to supply it in as many formats as you think you might need – for instance, zip, pdf, jpg and so on. Ideally you want to be able to use this material on your own computer, so discuss this with the designer and learn how to access these applications, if you don't already know.

Paper is cheap and the extra cost of good-quality paper or card is often small until you get to the ultra-expensive variety. Print your stationery on the best you can afford. Never compromise on the quality of materials for your business card as you want it to look crisp at all times and to survive being jammed into the pockets or bags of your contacts.

Website

You must have a website. It is now the main way that clients find or check out suppliers. At Management Futures, we have noticed the increasing frequency with which clients and prospective clients mention our website (www.managementfutures.co.uk). They do this in six ways, starting with the most frequent and ending with the least frequent:

1   They have already heard of us through some other means and use the website to check us out. If they like the look of what they see, they then email or call us.
2   They use the website to order books, course places or other materials.
3   They have already decided to work with us and use the website to endorse the decision. This is consistent with research into advertising which shows that car advertisements are read most carefully by people who have already bought the car.
4   They need to visit or contact us and use the website to check the address, map, email and phone number.
5   They are researching coaching or organizational development and have found us through a search engine.
6   They like our website and revisit to see what there might be on it of interest.

What is a website for?

First and foremost it gives clients a flavour of what it would be like working with you. By what you say about yourself and how you say it, you will convey who and what you are. It allows you to distinguish yourself from competitors. This is why it is not a good idea to copy the websites of other coaches – apart from anything else, so many just repeat the same old mistakes.

The website tells clients what problems you can solve for them and why they should work with you. It gives information about where they can contact you. As your business grows, you may also want to use it to sell products as well as coaching services.

Domain name

It is essential to have a proper domain name. Don't use Hotmail, AOL, Yahoo or any of the other free hosting services. It looks too homely. Look for a domain name which ideally is identical to the name of your business and is offered by a heavyweight Internet Service Provider (ISP). Look for an address which ends in .com, .co.uk, or any of the other so-called Top Level Domains (TLDs). Check this out on any of the many sites which will give you advice and registration by entering the words *domain registration* on Google or any other favourite search engine. You may find that your top preference has been taken, in which case the site will be able to suggest alternatives. Keep the address easy to spell. The longer it is, the more likely spelling mistakes are to creep in when people type in the words. Your website address needs to be linked to your email address. Mine is Jenny.Rogers@managementfutures.co.uk. So if clients know my email address they can also guess the website address and vice versa.

Design and content

Keep it simple in the early days. These guidelines will help:

- Quick downloading is essential. Clients will not wait for what will feel like aeons while your favourite graphics download, and many of them may not have the browsers which enable rapid downloading anyway.
- Bear in mind that reading from a computer screen is different from reading a book. For a start the format is landscape, not portrait, and it is far more difficult to scan quickly. Your copy needs to be short, sharp and simply written. It needs to attract attention immediately and be effortless to absorb. Think high-quality tabloid rather than doughy broadsheet. This is not your big authorial moment. Rein in any attempt to write tortuously complex articles. No one will read them: statistics suggest that at least two thirds of site visitors never get beyond the home page.
- Four or five pages is enough for a small business. You can add more later as your business expands.
- Make sure that all the links work and that you have rigorously excluded all typos. We employ a freelance copy editor to check our site frequently. It is amazing how many mistakes can creep in, and you, the author, are probably the last person to spot them. If your site contains typos and misspellings, what sort of impression does that give of your professionalism?
- Include a *contact-us* link which creates an instant email for enquirers.

- *Offer links* to any other websites you think might interest your clients.
- Your *home* page should include your name, your postal address and postcode, a map reference link (for instance, in Britain to street-map.co.uk), fax, email details and phone numbers.
- Your *customer* page should define the clients you work with and ideally will contain testimonials from satisfied customers.
- Your *people* page will include your biography – and you can include a photograph here – plus those of any partners or regular associates.
- The *services* page will list the services you provide and the benefits they bring.
- Finally, it is a good idea to give people a reason to visit your site other than just to gather information. A newsy piece or a free offering of some kind will help. For instance, you might offer tips on managing stress, or a guide to bringing up teenagers – depending on the market you are targeting.
- Aim to update the site at least once every six weeks.

Make sure that you include your web address on all your stationery and on any other materials associated with your operation.

It is possible to buy cheap software to create a site yourself or to teach yourself how to do it from scratch. There are many excellent web designers out there and for a relatively modest fee you will be able to buy something much better than you could design yourself and for a lot less trouble. Bear in mind that you will also need to maintain the site, so forming a good relationship now with the right designer will pay dividends over time. Exactly the same principles apply to a web designer as to choosing a graphic designer for your stationery. This may be the same person – many of the same skills apply. As with your choice of graphic designer, ask the same questions and look at other sites that your potential supplier has designed. Don't give the job to an amateur. When the inevitable differences of opinion emerge, it may be hard to disagree and even harder to insist on revamps or on deadlines being met. You need a proper professional relationship and this is much more likely when real money changes hands.

Newsletters

A newsletter, or its internet version an e-zine, is a way of telling your clients that you are still in business and that you value the relationship with them. At Management Futures we have produced a newsletter from the start. It now runs to 12 pages and we send it out three times a year. It is professionally written, designed and printed and consistently produces unsolicited positive feedback from our clients. From the start we worked from these principles:

It is not about overt selling but about giving, though we have always used it to announce new services and products.

We offer material that clients will find useful and want to keep.

It has a contemporary feel.

It reflects our values, not least our belief that while we take our work seriously, we do not take ourselves too seriously, so every edition has jokes and cartoons. These can sometimes get us into trouble – for instance, we ran a column called Politically Incorrect for a number of editions and some people did not see the joke.

There is a strong emphasis on human interest, with case studies and individual experience.

We archive the material on the website so that it has a dual use.

It reflects our clients' interests and concerns and is never about ourselves, except in passing. So you will never see a photograph of the happy Management Futures team on their summer day trip to Calais because we know that is of entirely nil interest to clients.

The purpose of our newsletter is to maintain the relationship with our clients and to remind them about us. Even though it is not an overt selling tool, we always notice a surge in sales and enquiries immediately after it goes out.

You would not have to produce something as complicated as our newsletter to achieve similar effects. I have seen several simple four-pagers written and distributed by successful coaches two or three times a year and they serve the same purpose. The most successful newsletters offer genuine added value to clients. For instance, they may update clients on some aspect of the law that has changed, or on the outcomes of interesting research they have conducted, or simply be a list of good-quality hints and tips relevant to their clients' lives. However, like a brochure, a newsletter is a major commitment. It has to be written, edited, designed, printed, proof-checked, stuffed into an envelope, labelled with accurate addresses, franked and taken to the post office. Your mailing list needs to be kept constantly up to date, and as it expands this will become an ever more onerous task. You need to be clear that the costs of creating it will be outweighed by delivering the benefits you are seeking.

Brochures

This is often the first investment that a new coach makes. My advice is to avoid this cost in your first few years.

> Your offer is likely to change significantly as you and your market respond to what your customers actually buy, as opposed to what you believe they might buy.

> All your competitors will be saying similar things about themselves. It is hard to differentiate yourself through a brochure.

> When a brochure has to be posted, this increases the cost per copy by a considerable margin.

> Websites have replaced print as the easiest way to get information about a company and the distribution costs are low by comparison.

> When clients ask you if you have something in print about yourself that you can send them, a simpler two-sheet statement may fit the bill equally well and will also be a lot more flexible.

If you do decide to create a brochure, the classic design principles apply. No brochure is read with as much time and attention as was given to it by its creator. You can expect a skim read, if that. No one ever made a coaching purchase on the basis of a brochure. The most it does is to encourage the potential client to ask for more information. So for all these reasons, it is better to keep any brochure to essentials with clear information, simply written and surrounded by generous white space. Don't be tempted to over-elaborate. One coaching company created a brochure which contained many magnificent black and white photographs taken by a seriously talented photographer. The paper was hand made with deckled edges and the photographs were so beautiful, each was protected by a transparent sheet. The impact was to ask, *What have these photographs got to do with coaching?* (*Nothing* was the answer), followed by *What on earth did this cost?* quickly followed (if you were a prospective client) by, *My fee would be paying for all this!*
The best brochures will usually follow this format:

> Clear designation of your target client.

> Solutions-focused descriptions describing the benefits your work offers to clients.

> A just-right amount of gloss in terms of paper and design.

A list of the organizations you have as clients – brief case studies may be appropriate as long as you can easily update them and you have the clients' permission.

All your contact details.

If you still feel that a brochure would be useful, work out the sums: design + print + distribution divided by number of copies = ? per copy. Is it worth it?

When you do decide to have a brochure, the easiest way to do it is to hold it on your computer and to print off copies a few at a time, as and when you want them. This will also enable you to produce targeted brochures for different markets.

Mail shots

A mail shot can be done through conventional postage or through email. If you get a 1 per cent reply-rate from a mail shot you are doing well, so you have to weigh up where the effort will pay off. For a start-up coaching business, there may be a number of situations where a mail shot is useful:

Announcing that you are open for business: a letter to all your contacts. Note that a real letter, and not junk mail, sent through the post now has considerable impact because it is relatively rare.

Announcing a new product or event, perhaps with a special offer for early birds.

You can increase the chances that your letter will be read and acted on by addressing the envelope by hand – that way the addressee will not confuse it with junk mail. End your mail shot with a clear 'call to action' – that is inviting the client to do something as a result of having read the letter. Alternatively, describe how you intend to follow it up – for instance with a phone call. Also, although it is a tired old marketeer's trick, research seems to show that a PS is read more carefully than anything else in the content. Otherwise, all the same principles of copy-writing apply.

Promotional methods once you are established

You might consider these approaches once you have an established business. They are unlikely to be worth the time, effort and money they cost in the early days.

Media exposure

All clients are sophisticated people, well aware that the aim of marketing materials is to sell, however softly the pitch is made. When you write a piece for your local paper, contribute an advice column in a magazine, or do a regular live phone-in for your local radio station, you have editorial endorsement. You will get double value from this – not only the exposure to a target audience, but also something worth including in your brochure or in other material. This is always going to be worth a great deal more than buying advertising space.

It takes time and persistence to find the right outlet. All editors have more people competing for space than there is space or airtime to give them. Approaches that work will always start with an in-depth understanding of their reader or listener/viewer profile. This needs to be a close match to your own target group. If it isn't, you are wasting your time. Once you have this data, find out who the commissioning editor is for the sort of slot or article you have in mind. It's always better to phone first. Emails and letters are likely to be ignored. Where you are still building your reputation and have limited writing or broadcasting experience, it is probably safer and easier to start modestly – for instance with a specialist professional journal or a very local paper where there will be less competition.

With writing assignments, remember that there is no greater sin to a journalist than missing a deadline. The second sin is delivering more than your assigned number of words. Keep strictly to your allocation. If you don't, you will discover that your piece is ruthlessly and not necessarily sensitively edited for you.

Being quoted as an expert

How do you get into a journalist's contacts book? This is unlikely to be easy unless you are already moving in the media world. The best way to do it is to look for public exposure through speaking at conferences, and writing books and articles.

Advertising

Coaching is not a commodity. A commodity is a product that you buy on price or convenience, where one product is to all intents and purposes just like another, or seems as if it is. When you are selling a commodity, one of the few ways you can make your product appear different from its rivals is by its physical packaging and through advertising. This is why the bulk of television advertising is for commodities, not for products that are already differentiated. Ask yourself if you would ever choose your own coach on the basis of an advertisement. I think the answer is that it is most unlikely. So don't waste your money on adverts. They are expensive and have a low chance of resulting in work. The exception might be where you are operating in a sector or location where it is clear that you can reach your target clients through some medium that is read by everyone – for instance, a free local newspaper or a magazine that is the only place where jobs in that sector are advertised. Once you grow your business, there is a modest case to be made for using advertising, placed shrewdly in targeted publications or websites, to familiarize clients with your brand, or to promote specific events, but at the early stages it will most probably not justify its costs.

Absolute essentials

You can add other elements later as your business grows. For the first few years these will be enough:

- A business name that sums up your offer.
- A set of professionally designed graphic images that convey the essence of your business.
- An attractive business card.
- A professionally designed website updated every six weeks.
- Writing about benefits, not coaching processes.

---

4 Presenting Yourself to Clients

The most powerful ways of attracting attention to your offer are the ones that put you in direct contact with potential clients, especially the clients who can make the critical decision about whether to take you on or not. This chapter is about how to make these methods work for you.

When you are face to face, clients have far richer experience of you than they could obtain from reading a brochure or a letter. You can have a dialogue, you can adapt, begin to develop a relationship, or continue an existing one. The more remote you are from the prospective client, the less likely it is that you will be able to make a sale. This seems obvious once stated, yet I have known many dozens of coaches who have relied entirely on the relatively passive methods of mail shots, brochures or websites and have then been deeply disappointed to find that no action results.

Your two-sentence summary

This is one of the simplest, most useful and most direct methods ever. You develop a smoothly rehearsed and pithy answer to the question: *What do you do?*

Imagine you are in your local pub and an acquaintance asks you this question. The acquaintance may be very slightly drunk and is only vaguely interested in your answer. It has to be concise enough to capture his or her attention and accurate enough to convey the essence of what you do. When you work in a standard job or in a big organization it is easy enough to answer the question by naming your job role: *I'm an accountant; I'm a PA; I'm a police officer; I'm the sales director; I'm a physiotherapist; I run the training department.* This does not work with coaching because it is still far from a mature market and saying you work as a coach will most probably leave many people as mystified as they were before they asked the question. Also you are missing one of the best and simplest ways of promoting your offer. So all coaches need to have a ready answer to this question because you will be asked it again and again. Take it as given that no one is going to be interested in a long recital of why you are in coaching, your coaching philosophy and your complete autobiography.

One easy way to develop your two-sentence summary is to use this protocol, based on the thinking you will already have done on your target markets:

I work with <description of typical target client>

on finding solutions to <describe typical problems>

and the benefits clients get from working with me are <describe the benefits>

Here are some real-life examples:

I coach people who appear on radio and TV. Through the coaching they learn how to give a clear, confident message – and on their terms.

I work with people who need new jobs and I help them to find their ideal job fast.

I help couples in troubled relationships to move on as happily as possible, either through saving the relationship or, if it has to end, with minimal turbulence, especially for their children.

My coaching is with senior partners in legal and accountancy firms, mostly in the north-west of England. We work on establishing the leadership style which will produce maximum results for their firms and for them.

I help outstanding people fast-track their careers.

I work with Chief Executives and Directors in public sector organizations. The emphasis is on how to develop a leadership style which creates commitment from the people around you and also ensures that your organization hits targets imposed from outside.

At this point offer the enquirer your business card. You never know ...

Dress

Image is important. You have an image whether you like it or not, just by what you choose to wear on any given day. If you have never had professional style and colour advice, I strongly advise you to do so, men and women alike. It's not about 'fashion', it's not about being a clone, nor is it a trivial topic. How you look – just as how your business card or brochure looks – is one of the main ways you can quickly convey the essence of who you are to a client. Within seconds of meeting you, a potential client will have summed you up. Do you look fit and healthy? Are you smartly dressed? Do you seem open and friendly? Is there anything weird or discordant about you? We judge all of these things on the flimsiest of criteria, but make no mistake, we judge.

In our company, we are frequently approached by people who want to work with us as associates. When their CVs seem interesting, we will ask them to come in to meet us. This is apparently just a friendly chat. The shrewd potential associate knows that it is actually the beginning of a mutual selection process, however deceptively informal it may seem. So we were not impressed by the woman who turned up wearing scuffed shoes, a strong whiff of stale talcum powder, a dress at least 15 years old and with its hem falling down. If your appearance seems generally sloppy, this suggests at the least a lack of self-awareness and possibly self-neglect, and if the coach is not self-aware and does not manage herself well, what credibility will she have with clients? If her clothing does not look contemporary, the same might be true of her thinking.

Here is how some other coaches deal with this issue:

> If I am aiming to attract advertising or media clients, I go for smart casual. I have learnt that their apparently laid-back dress is more calculated than it seems. For instance, they may be wearing jeans, but the jeans will be a premier brand and the polo shirt is from Paul Smith.

> I choose a formal but bright jacket if I'm going to a conference. I know from experience that there will be a sea of navy, grey and black and I want to stand out.

> I do match the formal suits, cuff links and sober ties of my clients in one particular organization, but where they tend to wear white or cream shirts, I make sure mine are subtle pastels and my tie is just a little more adventurous. That way I'm saying, *hey guys, I'm like you – but enough unlike to be interesting.*

Whatever style statement you want to make, you will want to suggest the self-awareness and self-confidence which add up to relaxed authority. The most important discriminator is therefore to choose high status rather than low status as your theme. These are the guidelines suggested by my colleague Jennifer Aston (page 25)

Women

High status is suggested by:	Low status is suggested by:
Structured styles These will have some tailoring, with at least some definite shape at the shoulders. Linings will help preserve shape.	*'Natural' styles* Floppy, unstructured, loose clothing.
Definite colours But these should be the right colours for you: get advice on this.	*Dressing to disappear* Please-don't-notice-me 'safe' and invisible colours.
Hair Immaculately cut, conditioned and coloured.	*No-style hair* Wash 'n' go appearance, e.g. wild curls, straggly or shapeless look, badly dyed or no thought to colour.
Light day make-up Women who wear discreet make-up look healthier and livelier. Research suggests that they get promoted far more often than women who don't.	*No make-up* All blemishes visible.
Keeping covered	*Stripping off* Bare legs, arms, cleavage, feet.

Men

High status is suggested by:	Low status is suggested by:
Immaculate grooming	*Grubby grooming* Clothes shiny from over-wear or urgently in need of dry cleaning/ laundering. BO. Dandruff on collar, stains on tie.
Quality clothes in good condition	*Cheap, poor-quality clothing in shabby condition*, e.g. crumpled shirts, unpressed trousers, frayed or curling collars.
Smart shoes, well polished	*Shoddy shoes*
Elegant collar and tie	*Distracting collar and tie*, e.g. in-your-face ties, knot too big or too small; collar wrong shape for face.
Up-to-date accessories	*Yesterday's accessories*

You may feel that you know all of this and that it is patronizing to have it pointed out. If so, then congratulate yourself on your wisdom. And of course such look-ism is unfair and ideally you should never judge people on outward appearance. But unfortunately, human beings make snap judgements because often there is too little time or willingness to make more measured ones. Dressing for high status does not win you the work, but if you are dressing in a way that suggests low status, you will make it harder for yourself.

Networking

The very word *networking* can evoke strong shudders of distaste. *It sounds like brown-nosing. It's self-serving. It's pointless. It's boring.* I have heard all these excuses from beginner coaches.

Networking and luck

The better connected you are, the luckier you are likely to consider yourself to be – and maybe the luckier you actually are – in a business as well as in a personal role. There are obvious business and social benefits to having a large network. The bigger your network, the more likely you are to:

   have people to turn to when something goes wrong; ask for and get support;

   be able to float ideas with others, thus getting thumbs up for good ideas, thumbs down for silly ones;

   make 'lucky' chance encounters and stay connected with the *zeitgeist*;

   be alerted early to new ideas in your areas of interest;

   get early warning of new trends in your sector; hear who is moving jobs; be aware of whose power is growing, whose is waning;

   find a life or business partner and friends;

   get feedback on positives and negatives about your style and thus be more realistic about yourself, neither overly self-congratulatory nor overly pessimistic.

How do you tell if you have a large enough network?

One study run by Hertfordshire University correlates luckiness with how many people you know on first name terms from each of 15 surnames. (For more information, see www.luckfactor.co.uk) In this study, 65 per cent of people knew someone with the most common name, Wilson, versus only 15 per cent who knew someone with the least common name on the list, Byrne. People who did not consider themselves either lucky or unlucky scored on average 6. Lucky people scored 8 or more and unlucky people 5 or fewer. Only eight of the 4000 people who took part claimed to know someone with all 15 names. Women knew significantly more people than men.

How many do you know? (Alternative spellings of the same name allowed.) Names are in order of best to least known.

The surname	The person you know on first name terms with this surname
Wilson	
Williams	
Walker	
Thomas	
Taylor	
Scott	
Ryan	
Roberts	
Reid	
Moore	
Hughes	
Davies	
Campbell	
Baker	
Byrne	
Total	

What is your own total? How adequate does the result suggest your current network is?

The favour bank

I see networking rather differently from its usual negative connotations. At Management Futures we have a concept that we call *generous networking*. We see it principally as an opportunity to give rather than to take. What can you offer your network? Which people could you connect? What useful ideas could you promulgate?

Another way of looking at networking is to compare it to banking principles where the currency is favours. The favour can be information, a task, advice, a recommendation. You do a favour for someone else, and you have credit in your account. They do a favour for you and they have credit in theirs. Each side may make withdrawals over a period of time. As long as there is a rough balance in the account, it works well for both sides. The favour bank is at its most useful when it operates outside your immediate professional environment because this is where you will hear of people, information and ideas beyond the daily exchange of information in your environment. If you do not have a favour bank, it is unlikely that you are networking effectively.

Where should you network?

You can waste a great deal of time at the wrong events. There are two kinds of networking occasions you should consider in building your business

events where you can meet potential clients;

events where you can meet other coaches.

Many beginner coaches do a great deal more of the second than of the first because they feel on safer ground. Meetings of other coaches are useful but they have a different purpose: your professional development. Unless you are hoping to develop a business as a coach-supervisor, you will not find new clients this way.

There is an endless menu of events where you can meet potential clients: business clubs, special-interest groups which meet regularly, conferences, seminars, parties and celebrations.

Before devoting time to attending an event with potential for networking, ask yourself these questions:

How many of my typical target clients will be attending?

Do I already know at least one person likely to be there so that I can manage any initial shyness?

How well connected are the typical attendees? For instance, a local business club may be too small in itself to generate many clients, but if the people who do attend are influential, they may be able to smooth your path to other potential clients – assuming that you want to develop local business.

Will the likely cost, time and energy I will expend justify the benefits I am likely to obtain?

How much am I likely to benefit professionally in terms of updating myself on trends in my market?

Will I enjoy meeting the people who will be there? The answer to this question should definitely be *yes*. If you don't actually like your typical target client then you are aiming at the wrong market.

Fear of rejection

Dismissing the value of networking is usually about fear and sometimes about lacking the technique and skill to work a room. All of the negative self-talk that we do when faced with a room of people whom we don't know has its roots in fear of rejection: the ultimate punishment for herd animals. However, our excuses don't stand up to any real scrutiny:

The excuse	*The reality*
You can't talk to someone if you haven't been introduced	You don't need to wait for someone to introduce you – you can introduce yourself
I'm shy	Shyness is a form of self-absorption. Think of your role as being to put other shy people at their ease
I've got nothing to say to people I don't know	As a coach you know how to ask the questions that emphasize your interest in the *other* person
You shouldn't be pushy – who'd want to talk to me? All these people are more important and interesting than I am	Other people could be feeling just the same, but it takes a good networker to break the ice

Cures for networking aversion

Prepare

Who will be there? Who would it be intriguing and interesting to get to know? What benefit might there be in talking to them? What background research might you do to find out something about them in advance? When you are at a conference, scrutinize the delegate list and highlight the people you would like to meet. Take plenty of business cards.

See yourself as a host, not a guest

This is the major transformation in attitude that will help. A guest waits patiently to be introduced, hangs back, needs to be looked after. A host does the opposite: takes the initiative, introduces him- or herself, introduces people to each other, ferries food and drink. This rule applies to any gathering, regardless of whether you are formally the host. As a host, you are concerned with others, not with yourself.

Implications

- At a table of 'strangers' take on the host role: introduce yourself and ask everyone round the table to do the same.
- Act as the 'introducer' at a conference or party; take the initiative and move people around, especially if you see that someone is on their own or has got stuck for what looks like a long time with the same person.
- Breaking out of solo: look for trios rather than pairs to break into. Pairs may be having an intense conversation which could involve a business deal, a flirtation or a reconciliation. Trios are unlikely to be so preoccupied. Join the trio. Join in at first with *nods* and other attentive body language. Make direct eye contact with one of the trio. Wait for a brief pause in the conversation, then introduce yourself and make some contribution to the discussion, depending on what you have just heard.
- Be prompt – and stay a reasonable amount of time at the whole event. It's a cop-out to arrive late and leave early.
- Beware of over-eagerness to do business. Networking is a social process. Follow up with serious business propositions later, e.g. with an email, phone call or letter. Ask permission to do this:
  I'll write to you if I may, when I'm back in the office.

Ending the conversation

- Don't overstay your welcome – the point of a party or a conference is to mingle.
- Move away when you've finished something you're saying rather than after the other person has been speaking. Give the person your business card; offer your hand again and say something like, *It's been really pleasant to meet you – I hope you enjoy the rest of the event*, then leave cleanly.
- Move at least a quarter of the room away.
- Say, *I'm ready for some food/another drink – are you?* If your offer of a fresh drink is accepted, bring it and then move off straight away, using one of the lines of dialogue below.
- Say, *Anyway* ... letting the word trail away. This is universally recognized in the UK as a signal that the conversation is over.
- Say, *I need to find <the loo; person X; the conference organizer; my colleague>* and say goodbye as above.
- Take the person with you to meet someone else, then leave them chatting with the new person.

For further useful and practical ideas, consult Susan RoAne's book, *How to Work a Room* (2000).

Networking is a long-term investment in your time and energy. Here is a friend and former colleague describing how she started a coaching practice in a totally new country. To make the challenge even more daunting, this is also a Middle-Eastern country where coaching itself is not widely understood.

> *Louise Coates*
>
> My aim when we moved to Dubai eighteen months ago was to set up a coaching practice, spreading the word about the benefits of coaching whilst building a personal reputation as the *must-see woman if you want to get on in your career*. In my business plan I gave myself three months to settle in to the new culture and make contacts, then I hoped the work would start to flow.
>
> It didn't quite go that way. For a start I found that many HR managers who had been away from Europe or the US whilst the revolution of coaching has been raging still equated coaching with training. With that assumed link came the notion of pricing – at a fraction of a day's training fee.
>
> Only slightly dented in resolve, I made use of the spare time to put myself about – attending almost any sort of networking event that presented itself. International Businesswomen's Group, Dubai HR Forum, writers' groups, the lot. I made contact with coaching groups in other parts of the world who might have been interested in a local partner. I gave talks at events, wrote articles for the regional HR magazine and ran introductory workshops. I talked to a number of organizations that may have benefited from a coaching partner.
>
> The break came from one of the early contacts, requesting that I coach one of his senior managers. Another contact asked if I could help prepare some of his managers for attending a prestigious European programme. Gradually more referrals came through the contacts I had made. I became succinct in response to the question *and what do you do?* I'd reply, *I keep managers on the fast track*.
>
> There are still busy times and slow times. The networking has paid off many times over in social terms as well as business contacts. I have also come across a surprising number of other professional coaches and together we have set up a support group and marketing website. Soon every organization here will know about coaching, and me.

Talks and conferences

When you speak at a conference, or give a talk at your local business club, you immediately assume some of the authority associated with the event or the sponsoring organization. They have chosen you, so you must be good. The more respected the sponsor, the more likely this is to be true. The assumption is that you have something interesting to say.

Exactly the same principles apply here as to every other marketing tool. A presentation or talk will only be useful if you are talking to the right people about topics that interest them. You must be able to speak entertainingly and fluently. If you can't, then it will pay you to get a voice or presentation coach yourself, or to join Toastmasters, a non-profit-making organization devoted to better public speaking, where frequent practice and copious feedback can have dramatic impact on performance (www.toastmasters.org). Formats that work will nearly always include your top tips on whatever topic the audience is concerned about, well illustrated with human interest anecdotes. An intriguing title will help ensure that you get a good audience. You might notice, also, how often an experienced presenter includes a number in his or her title. I learnt from this myself, so I called one of my own recent talks *Seven Well-Known Secrets of Managing Change*. I have also given conference presentations entitled *Ten Ways to Lead a Balanced Life*.

Some coaches worry that by giving a talk they will be giving away their secrets. This is a groundless concern. First, there is no such thing as a secret – this is why I called my talk *Seven Well-Known Secrets*, because I made a point of saying that everyone already knew most of what I was going to say. What is interesting is why they don't act on it – the very area in which coaching works. Secondly, what people remember from talks is how they were given. The content is quickly forgotten.

The best way to get a platform is to make it a priority for developing your business and to ask for invitations directly. Approach any of your most senior contacts and ask them when they are next running a conference. Ask for an introduction to the conference organizer. Use selling skills (see Chapter 5) to offer your idea. Another excellent method is to scan the professional journals to which you subscribe – and you will of course be taking out subscriptions for journals which feed your target market, and to note requests for papers at forthcoming conferences. Typically, you write a brief summary of the session you would run, using the promotional tools I have already discussed – for instance, making it clear what benefits would be obtained by the people who attend your session. A committee often scrutinizes these outline papers and there will be competition. A call to the organizers asking them what they are looking for and where there are gaps will often yield good results.

Be prepared to run a workshop or to do a plenary session. Big names on the conference circuit can command large fees, depending on the nature of their celebrity. Most coaches will not fall into this category. Don't expect to get paid anything other than your expenses or to be offered a free conference place or dinner – it is a bonus if you actually get a fee. You are speaking for recognition, not for money.

Conferencing is now big business and not only may you not be offered a fee, but you may also be asked to pay for the privilege of speaking. This is simply another form of sponsorship. It is obviously much better to earn your platform on your merits than to have to buy it, but the fact that such exposure is now sometimes for sale emphasizes its value. Large conferences also offer opportunities for briefer and more informal exposure – for instance chances to facilitate table discussions over lunch, where delegates can opt to join a table dedicated to a particular topic. Take these opportunities when they occur – often they are arranged at the last minute.

If a conference as such sounds too grand and daunting, small local chapters of specialist groups can be equally good places to find clients. They are easier to penetrate, especially if you already belong to them. Approach the events secretary and offer to run a session.

Presentations with impact

To get maximum leverage from any session where you speak, whether a conference or a more informal event:

- Ask yourself who the typical attendee will be, what problems they have and how coaching could provide solutions.
- Keep the prepared part of your talk brief: 20 to 25 minutes maximum. That is the longest time you can expect people to concentrate.
- You want people to listen to you, rather than read what you are saying from a screen, so keep slides to a minimum and with no more than 45 words on each. Work without them if you can.
- If you do use slides, have your website details on each one.
- A presentation is a performance: get feedback on how well you do.
- Always include an interactive element where people can ask lively questions or do some kind of small-group activity.
- Consider doing some kind of live coaching demonstration.
- Put some printed material on every seat – for instance, a one-page summary of your talk with all your contact details clearly printed at the top.
- Say that you will offer a free introductory coaching session to the first two people who ask.
- Negotiate with the conference organizer to be given the email contact details of every attendee and follow up each one with some

further goodie – for instance, more detailed material on the subject of your talk.

- Exchange business cards with the people who come up to talk to you at the end of your presentation and follow them up with phone calls after the event.
- Don't talk about coaching processes: talk about outcomes and benefits with illustrative anecdotes.
- Do no overt selling at all.

Breakfast seminars

The meetings could be lunches or suppers but the breakfast slot feeds the popular fantasy that we are all far too busy to break into the flow of our working days. However, we may be persuaded to start it with peers, as long as we feel we are going to get some practical benefit from it and can vaguely justify it as *work* to cynical colleagues. Breakfast is also a simple meal and the cost of providing it is modest compared to the cost per head of meals where alcohol or more elaborate food is expected.

Note that you can probably only do this if you are operating from a metropolitan area where you have a big enough catchment area of clients and where travel time and hassle for your potential guests is minimal. This is how it works. You identify roughly twenty times more people than you actually want to attend. The majority should be people with whom you already have some contact. So if you aim to have ten guests, you will need to invite 200 people. If you receive 16 acceptances, you can guarantee that six will be no-shows – they got delayed, something more interesting came up the day before, or it was raining and they couldn't be bothered. You choose a pleasant, central venue and you lay on a simple breakfast with wonderful croissants and warm rolls, maybe some cold meats and cheese, beautiful jams, fresh fruit, coffee, tea and juice.

The invitation will have offered them some desirable benefit: a new insight into a common problem, the results of some recent research, a set of how-to's, a practical response to a new piece of legislation, an updating on thinking relevant to their worlds. After 15 minutes of useful networking with each other, you and your guests sit down to breakfast. When everyone is on their second cup of coffee, you make your presentation. All the rules of giving good conference performances apply equally here except that a breakfast seminar is a lot more informal and your own talk needs to be short – maybe 15 minutes at most, followed by discussion rather than just the question-and-answer routine more suited to large groups. Make sure that people have some kind of practical take-away – for instance, a useful handout. The whole thing is over in two hours. You follow up with phone calls or emails, as appropriate.

The difference from a conference is that a breakfast seminar is an invitation-only event. It is small-scale, friendly and focused. It is an occasion for you to serve your clients by offering them something they cannot get elsewhere. It is about the relationship, not about selling. When clients do mention that they might have a need for coaching, for themselves, for their company or for a colleague, make it firm policy that you do not discuss it at the seminar. Tell them warmly and courteously that you will contact them as soon as possible at a mutually convenient time – and fix the time then and there.

Offering free or ultra-cheap sessions

When you are at the absolute beginning of building a practice, one of the best ways to find paying clients is to offer free sessions. This may seem paradoxical, but it has worked for many dozens of the new coaches we train. Once you have coached six or seven clients, you can add anonymized descriptions of them to your marketing materials because it matters not a jot whether or not they paid for their sessions. It works best if:

> You are totally candid with these clients about your need for experience and quotable track record.

> It is clear that coaching on these terms is a one-off and temporary – it's an *introductory offer*.

> You explain that it is part of your training and/or start-up phase – this makes it obvious that after a given period you will work at the professional rates normal in your field.

> Assuming that they are delighted with your work, the explicit *quid pro quo* is that you ask these clients to recommend you to others and also ask if you may use their names with other potential clients.

On the basis that what we get completely free, we tend not to value, some beginners like to make a nominal charge for this work. Another variant is that the first three sessions are free but that you charge proper rates for subsequent ones. Depending on the field you are choosing, the best way to find these free clients is a direct approach. Put the word about in your social network if you are going into life coaching, or call senior contacts in organizations if you will be working in the executive coaching field. Yet another variant here is to ring your contacts and discuss how far coaching could be useful in his or her organization and to offer a pilot programme on free or cheap terms, to be evaluated by both of you after it is completed.

Barter

This is another possibility. Informal bartering may occasionally be useful. One of the best barters I ever did was with the talented architect Mary Lou Arscott, who had her coaching in return for redesigning my then garden. That architect's work turned out to be so special that she later (this time on non-barter terms, of course) turned a concrete shell into a beautiful apartment for us and later still, and even more spectacularly, a whole house built on a heritage site in Norfolk (www.knoxbhavan.com). Barter depends on you and your potential client having something that you each genuinely want to exchange. Fixing the exchange value can be tricky and that is why it is a relatively rare transaction where services are involved.

Getting referrals

There are two ways this can work: building partnerships with other companies and getting referrals from influential individuals.

Strategic partnerships

One of the most effective ways to find new clients is to build partnerships with other professionals whose client base and area of operation is distinctly different from your own. These people will refer clients to you and you will refer clients to them.

We have several of these informal partnerships. One is with Re-Act, a company specializing in supplying actors to work with corporate clients (www.e-react.co.uk). An example of our joint work would be a project working with the National Deaf Children's Society and Professor Adrian Davies of Manchester University to train medical professionals who have to give parents the sobering and painful news that their baby is profoundly deaf. The actors role-play the parents and coach the professionals in their communication skills, working with our staff. As part of the *quid pro quo*, we have trained most of Re-Act's key associates as coaches at low or no cost because we want such associates to be able to work side by side with our own staff in ways that are consistent with our own values and practices.

Some obvious places to look, depending on the market you are in, could be your own professional advisers – your lawyer, doctor, accountant, financial planning adviser. Others could include firms who are in a parallel but different market – for instance, companies that train but do not coach, or companies that do consulting but not coaching.

What makes for a good strategic partner?

The most potentially useful strategic partners will have these characteristics:

Understand what coaching is – ideally because they have personally benefited from it.

Understand and are in touch with your target market.

Share your values.

Are not competitors.

Have expertise which you do not have and from which your own clients could benefit and vice versa.

Are respected in their market place.

Can benefit from your referrals to them and want to continue to build their own businesses. Strategic partnerships do not work when potential partners are complacent about the current size of their business.

Are running successful businesses themselves. It does not work when potential partners are desperate: they will want more from you than you can give and if their own client base is shrinking, their endorsement could be valueless.

Making the relationship work

These relationships only work when each side has something to give and something to get. They are typically informal, not legalistic. But anything one-sided will eventually wither away. Start with a candid exploratory conversation and remember that at this stage you have nothing to sell and nothing to buy. You are just asking the right questions about common need. Once it is clear that there is indeed some mutual benefit to be gained, talk candidly about how the process might work. Money does not usually change hands. When you make a referral yourself, always contact the partner so that he or she knows to expect a call from the potential client and ask the partner to let you know what happens. Extend the same courtesy in return when the partner refers a potential client to you. Be generous. You are in it for the long haul, not for immediate profit. If this is not true for you then finding strategic partners will not work anyway.

Keep in touch regularly and involve the partner in professional and social events – for instance, inviting them to breakfast seminars and conferences, and to your own Christmas or summer parties. Review the relationship at least once a year, perhaps over dinner or a drink. If it seems to be getting one-sided, discuss what you might do to restore the balance. For instance, if you find yourself doing all the referring, the partner may actually have forgotten that it is supposed to be a two-way deal. Ask what he or she might do to refer clients to you and explore why this might not be happening and be willing to do the same yourself if the boot is on the other foot.

Influential enthusiasts

Former clients who are also influential people can be your best advocates. You will most probably notice that you have strong feelings of warmth and admiration for them. All are likely to be stars in their own worlds. For instance, one particular executive at the BBC has probably referred as many as twenty clients to me over the years and many of these clients have referred others, in turn. As her own career has thrived and she has become more senior, so her own sphere of influence has expanded and the level of seniority of the people she has referred to me has also risen.

All you need to do with this kind of person is to make it known that you would like to work with anyone they recommend. They will need nothing more in the way of a prompt. This is because people like this are not motivated by the kind of mutual business reward which characterizes the typical strategic business partner. Rather, they love connecting people. They adore recommending. They are enthusiasts who are also insightful about the likely needs of others. They hate to see someone floundering when they know how much coaching could help. Their contacts list would exceed the average person's many times over. They are influential in their worlds and appear to know everyone who matters. You cannot force a relationship on this kind of person because authenticity is what they are all about. But when you encounter them, especially when they have been your clients, prize them and be grateful that life has put them your way.

Cross-selling

Feeding your coaching practice through parallel activities

Few of the coaches whom I know make a living entirely from coaching. Almost all mix coaching with other activities such as facilitation, organizational development, interim management, advisory services of one kind or another, consulting and training. The virtue of this is that these other activities can feed you coaching clients and vice versa. This is because the skills are extremely similar – something clients can see for themselves. So if they have experienced you in action as a trainer or facilitator they will already know what it would be like to work with you. Training or facilitation also gives you pricelessly valuable opportunities to see a potential client in action and to offer them feedback on their personal style – something that is essential to effective coaching. It is usually obvious when a client could benefit from coaching.

Here are some examples of how various coaches approach the opportunities to cross-sell:

> Team coaching is one of my best ways of finding coaching clients. Whenever I am doing this work I am alert to who I might approach about building some coaching into the follow-up. For instance, many senior people are incredibly isolated and have no one to use as a sounding board – they have often already confided this to me in the preparatory stages. About half of the people I talk to this way become coaching clients, not always immediately, because sometimes it takes a further crisis to bring about the actual request.

> When we are tendering for organizational development work, we usually suggest coaching as one of the interventions on the assumption that this is one of the most powerful ways of getting the change messages to stick.

> Stress-management is one of my specialities but about half my time is spent on facilitation with teams. At any given awayday you can bet that there will be someone who is under acute stress. I will discreetly approach them, discuss what I have observed and describe how I think I might be able to help through coaching. There is a bit of suspicion sometimes that I am suggesting 'therapy' but I would say that about half of these conversations result in coaching work.

> I do a great many 360 feedback de-briefs for a particular company as part of a major training programme. I used to find them immensely frustrating because I only had 40 minutes with each person. You'd just be getting to the heart of the issues when the session was over. What I did that worked really well was to approach the company and suggest that it would be hugely beneficial for these people to have the option of further coaching. About half of them take it up.

> When you work with executive clients as their coach, you will also get to know a great deal about the organizational issues that perplex them, leading to requests to facilitate awaydays or to undertake team coaching.

These opportunities for cross-selling are not confined to the executive coaching field. For instance, a hypnotherapist specializing in smoking cessation will have opportunities to suggest life coaching to his or her clients. A financial services adviser may also have an interest in couple-coaching – and so on.

Be alert to these opportunities and don't be bashful about suggesting coaching to clients for the other services you offer and vice versa.

High-cost promotional methods

Exhibitions

Taking a stand at an exhibition may be a method of promotion to consider once your business is established, but be warned: it is expensive. Exhibitions often run parallel to conferences, so it might be worth taking a stand if you are also a speaker. Remember that you have to consider not only the cost of hiring the space but also how you will dress it, whether you need a helper, travel, accommodation, and the opportunity-cost of attending. Before committing yourself, ask these questions:

How many people actually attended the previous year's event?

How many of my core target clients are likely to be present at this exhibition?

Does the status and subject of the conference fit well with my own offer?

How many coaching engagements would I need to obtain to cover the costs?

Think about what you can do at the stand to attract attention. Just lolling around is boring and may also look pitifully desperate. To get around this awful prospect, we took a stand at an exhibition supporting a conference where we knew that many of our previous and existing clients were likely to be present. We asked for the stand to be constructed so that we could offer what we called Speed Coaching sessions – in effect mini-tasters, followed up later with an email. We kept a whiteboard on the stand where people could book the slots. This was popular and was more interesting to do than waiting for people to talk to us.

We have seen other tactics to attract attention work well at exhibitions. These have included: opportunities to learn juggling (this did have some alleged connection with coaching, but I'm afraid I forget what it was); trying out psychometric software; dipping fruit into a chocolate fountain. There is also the well-known tactic of entering a free raffle by dropping your business card into a bowl. The prize here could be a coaching package worth real money.

Cold calling

The *cooler* the prospective client (i.e. the less contact they have had with you and the less you know about them) the less likely this method is to work. All clients will also be on the receiving end of a stream of cold callers; indeed they are so frequent, and so annoying, that they now fall into the category of *nuisance calls*. Cold calling is a specialized marketing tool. You can make it work if you use the selling principles described in Chapter 5, especially if you are clear at the outset of the conversation that you are making a sales call. Even so, this is not a tactic for the fainthearted and you have to be prepared to work both hard and skilfully to get beyond the first few minutes.

Absolute essentials

- Rehearse and get feedback on your two-sentence summary about yourself.
- Dress for high status.
- Invest time in networking with potential clients.
- Look for opportunities to give talks.
- Offer free sessions to build your confidence and expand your client list.
- Cross-sell coaching through your other activities.

---

5 Selling

This chapter is about how to sell effectively and with integrity: something that a lot of coaches find challenging.

Salespeople were a welcome part of the rhythm of life in the quiet suburban area where I grew up. There was the fish van, the baker, the brush salesman who later added cleaning products to his wares, the Corona man, the scissors and knife sharpener, the insurance salesman and, later on, the Avon lady, among many others. I remember no hostility or anxiety about their visits. If you needed their products, you bought them. If you didn't, then you might need them another time and you parted on comfortable terms. Like most of our neighbours, we had no car and buying from the door was a convenient way to purchase at least some of what we needed.

No doubt there was plenty of less-than-perfect selling behaviour in those austere post-war times because, human greed being what it is, the dodgy salesperson has always been with us. But today, our affluence, the confusing surfeit of choice and the easy availability of information has made us simultaneously gullible and suspicious consumers, ever on the alert for a better buy, prey to I-want-it-now copy in magazines, yet also looking to repel unwanted advances from intrusive salespeople who use the telephone to invade our peace on Sundays, infiltrate our computers or stalk us in shops. We enjoy finding clever bargains at discount warehouses. We scrutinize the labels on our food. At an individual level we expect to be manipulated when we buy high-value items like houses and cars, so we play the haggling game with the seller.

No wonder so many coaches feel anxiety about selling. In the competitive world in which we operate, there will always come a point where we are talking directly with the potential client, either face to face or on the phone, and hoping to come away with the order. These are the main reasons that we can dread the selling process. They are all about fear:

Rejection.

Failure.

Letting down colleagues if we do not get the work.

Being obliged to use the tarnishing and morally flawed techniques of the high-pressure sales world.

Not making the sale goes with the patch – you cannot win every single time. But there is no need to worry about using selling techniques that are counter to coaching values. The sales techniques I describe in this chapter are entirely consistent with coaching values – indeed, use near-identical approaches.

Coaching principles and selling principles

At Management Futures we base our coaching work on six core principles. There is nothing unique or surprising in them and most coaches would endorse them:

1   Clients are resourceful. At some level they know the answers to their own problems though they may be uncertain about how to get there. The clients are the ones who will have to live with the consequences of any decisions they make, not the coach.
2   It follows from this that the coach's role is to work with the client to access that resourcefulness. It's not about giving advice. This is why the essence of an effective coach is someone who asks skilful questions rather than offering answers.
3   Coaching is about the whole person – you can't split off the work person from the private person, or vice versa.
4   Coaching works from the client's, not the coach's, agenda.
5   The coach and client are equals: it's a partnership based on mutual respect and trust.
6   Coaching is about identifying what changes will make positive improvements in the client's life and then implementing those changes.

This approach to coaching is based on deep and authentic respect for clients. It assumes that they can and will make good judgements and that our role is to help them do just that. As the renowned sports coach Dave Alred has remarked, *Great coaches manage learning, they don't give instruction.* Now let's apply this philosophy to selling. Here are six equivalent principles:

1   Clients know what problems they want to solve through buying but may still be uncertain of how to approach it. They only seek outside help when they have exhausted all the obvious remedies.
2   When you are selling coaching your role is to work with the client to facilitate the decision to buy. It's not about pushing your product (the selling equivalent of giving advice). So, exactly as in coaching, it's about asking questions, rather than giving answers.

3   It is liberating as a coach to realize that you do not have to find the solution on behalf of the client. It is equally liberating to realize that the less you try to sell (by offering your pre-packaged solution) and the more you concentrate on helping the buyer to buy, the more likely you are to make the sale.

4   The rest of the client's system is inevitably involved in making the decision to buy and part of your role as the seller is to help the buyer measure what impact the rest of that system is likely to have on the decision. You will never know as much about this as the buyer, but by standing outside it you can ask the questions which will help the buyer decide.

5   People buy using their own criteria, not the seller's criteria, just as in the actual coaching you are working from the client's agenda and from their criteria of success, not from yours.

6   Selling works best when it is based on an entirely non-manipulative approach and is a partnership of equals, based on mutual respect. The decision to buy emerges out of this partnership. Your role as the seller is to base everything you do on this assumption. This will include directness and honesty when what the clients want is not a good match to what you offer – and being prepared to say so.

My own approach and thinking on the subject of selling has been radically affected by reading the US author Sharon Drew Morgen's books. Sharon Drew is a former stockbroker turned sales training guru. Her whole philosophy is summed up by the title of one of her books, *Selling With Integrity*, and is based on her profound belief in the value of collaboration – in selling as in everything else. She calls her approach *Buying Facilitation*®. When I read her books I realized that when my selling had been successful I had, unknowingly, been using a virtually identical approach, and that when my attempts to sell had failed it was because I had fallen into what she calls *old paradigm* patterns. You can download an electronic version of *Buying Facilitation* direct from her website, *www.newsalesparadigm.com*, and I heartily recommend that you do.

When selling fails

When coaching fails it is always because the six principles have not been honoured and one of the chief reasons is that coaches are more concerned to sell their pre-packaged solution than they are to listen and ask questions. When selling fails it does so for exactly the same reasons. It is always because sellers fail to create rapport (and remember that true rapport cannot be faked because it is based on respect and acceptance), think they know best, talk more than they listen and never understand how limited is their knowledge of the client's system. Old-style selling, including the approach known as *consultative selling* – also based on asking questions – is still essentially manipulative because it is designed to lead the buyer to what the seller thinks will be good for them. When you use the Buying Facilitation approach, in effect you do the opposite: you act as coach to your potential buyer on whether or not to buy you. It may feel counter-intuitive at first, but it works and it works fast.

Since encountering the Buying Facilitation method I have also realized that I have felt most satisfaction with a purchase when this is the method that has been used with me.

A car-buying example of poor and good practice

A few years ago I wanted to replace my car. I had been a Saab driver for six years. My loyalty had been somewhat strained by the comments of a colleague who had driven it on our way to give a paper at a conference. Driving it was, he said, 'like trying to pull a water buffalo out of a swamp'. While these comments were, let us say, just a little exaggerated and unfair, they set me thinking about whether I really wanted to take the lazy option and buy the same again.

I set up visits and test-drives at three car showrooms. At Saab, I was treated with the sort of superficial courtesy which masks stultifying indifference. The salesman's remarks started with comments about value for money and were addressed to my husband who was accompanying me because he couldn't think of anything better to do on a wet Saturday afternoon.

I had left my husband at home when I went to BMW. Here I was treated with enthusiasm, but most of the enthusiasm was for the car, especially for its performance on motorways. In fact I do far more city than motorway driving but by then could not be bothered to interrupt the flow of data about the car. The salesman chattered excitedly about what was under the bonnet, failing to notice my boredom and seemed surprised and defensive when I asked him about a recent case where a lone woman driving the exact same model had been hijacked on a motorway. The test drive was short.

At Audi, the salesman introduced himself in a friendly but not unctuous way, offering me a pleasantly firm handshake, addressed me as Mrs Rogers until I encouraged him to use my first name, maintained good eye contact and told me his name. It is Tim. I remember it because I later bought another car from him.

This is a shortened version of how the conversation went.

Tim: So I notice you're driving a Saab. How do you feel about that?
Jenny: Well, so-so. It's the second one I've had and I've always liked

them. It's been reliable but I've come to think that the acceleration is a bit slow and I'm wondering what else there is around.

Tim: Yes, Saab is certainly a good quality car and very reliable. [Brief conversation about what else I liked about the Saab.]
Is there anything else that's missing for you in how the car performs?

Jenny: Well, I'd like something that looks a bit sleeker and maybe has a better sound system because I get bored driving so I listen to music and to the radio a lot. And I don't know whether the Audi has a side impact safety system. Can you tell me if it does?

Tim: Yes, it does indeed. I can tell you anything you need to know about the car and the safety features, but first, if it's OK with you I'd like to hear a bit more about what you want. What's prompted the interest in replacing your current car?

Jenny: The Saab is nearly three years old and it's done its time for me, so I want to start afresh now. I get a bit twitchy about reliability and breaking down in city centres – most of my driving is in London and in heavy traffic.

Tim: Yes, breakdowns are dreadful wherever they happen – we all want to avoid that!

Jenny: The most important thing is reliability – I hate having my car off the road. Then it's got to feel good to drive – I can't be doing with cars where they feel heavy and awkward or give me backache. Then safety – I want all the gizmos going. It must be automatic because it will be driven occasionally by a disabled driver as well as by me.

Tim: Could you tell me a bit more about any other people who might drive it? Are you involving them in the actual choice?

Jenny: No, I would be the driver 90 per cent of the time so it's down to me. Oh – and the car door on the driver's side needs to open pretty wide so that the disabled driver can get in easily.

Tim: So you've already described reliability, safety, a good comfortable 'feel', a budget of £x, sleekness, auto gearbox, accessibility for the disabled driver, and a good sound system. Which of those is the most and least important for you?

Jenny: You've just described them – in that order!

Tim: Good. Well why don't we get into the car and do a test drive. It will take about 20 minutes, is that OK for you? Then you can get a feel for what it can do and how you like driving it – it'll be worth taking a bit of time, by the way, to get the driving position right before we start because that's what causes backache most of the time. I'll make sure we go somewhere you can test the acceleration. Have you got a favourite CD in your car that we can stick in the sound system? Excellent – so you can try that out too. Then when we get back, I can talk you through all the reliability and safety stuff.

Reader, I bought that car. In fact I had mentally bought it even before we got in for the test drive. The critically important behaviour and the one that secured the sale for him was that *this was a salesman who demonstrated greater interest in helping me make a good choice than he did in making the sale*. While clearly respecting the quality of the car he was selling, he did not rubbish the opposition. He addressed me with friendly formality but only used my name once, thus avoiding the toe-curling faux-intimacy of the salesman who has read his Dale Carnegie and believes that nothing creates more music in our ears than the frequent sound of our own first names. He listened more than he talked and did expert summaries throughout the conversation. He never at any stage told me what would be good for me, never once pressed me to buy or forced data on me. In fact, if you read the above carefully again, you will see that he positively avoided all traditional selling behaviours including politely postponing offering me facts, even when I asked for them. He established what the decision-making system was and he established my criteria. He did not bother me with technical data at all. *Objections* – the technical term for the *yes-butting* that a reluctant buyer puts up – never featured once in our conversation because there were none. The car easily met all my criteria and we quickly agreed a fair price.

In case you're wondering whether Tim's performance with me was a one-off, think again. He is a star. This selling behaviour works with everyone and it works with selling coaching as well as it works with selling cars.

Old and new selling behaviours contrasted

The difference between the approach to selling that I describe in this chapter and other approaches to selling is profound. In the older approach, still the dominant way that virtually all selling is done, product knowledge is everything. In coaching terms this would be the equivalent of being able to reel off the differences between life coaching, executive coaching and counselling without taking breath, or to describing what NLP is, or being able to spell out the superb benefits of your offer with articulacy and élan. Linked with this is the idea that the buyer does really need your product or service, but may be too dim to know it. So your role is to lead them, with spark and charm – it's a performance – to the point where they realize that there is a hole in their lives that can only be filled by your coaching.

Because buyers, even if allegedly *dim*, can see that this is what is happening, and do not therefore trust the salesperson, they create *objections – it's too expensive, I don't want to travel, I'm not ready yet*. The seller then has his or her rehearsed answers to the objections, because they are all familiar. Depending on what then happens, he or she tries to close the sale, often by haggling, or by creating a bogus sense of urgency – *I could start the coaching next week, but after that there's two months of a full diary.* (Sale finishes in only two days!!!) Or, *Well, if it's too expensive, I expect I could do a discount.* This is why in traditional sales training, the skills of negotiation are such an important part of the curriculum. At this point, the buyer's energy goes into wriggling free: *I'll let you know, send me a brochure, I've got other coaches to see* ... The whole exchange is characterized by the uneasy games-playing of hunter and hunted.

In the new approach, buyer and seller work in collaboration. The seller's role is to help the buyer to decide what he or she wants. Product knowledge is irrelevant at this stage. The essential skill is, as it is in coaching, *facilitative questioning*. Objections are irrelevant: when the questioning is done correctly, they are never raised. The relationship is one of mutual trust and candour. The seller works exclusively to the buyer's criteria and only offers product information when those criteria are clear and only sells to those criteria. The atmosphere is relaxed, though also pacey because it is one of discovery and may result in a sale which is pleasing to both sides. If it doesn't, both buyer and seller can walk away with self-esteem undamaged.

This table sums up the main differences:

	Old-style selling	**New-style selling**
Beliefs	Buyers too confused or stupid to know what they want. Look how often they say, *I don't know* ...	Buyers know what they need and with seller's help will identify it precisely
	Buyers can be bamboozled if you have enough skill and persistence	Buyers know manipulation when they see it. They appreciate directness and honesty
Skills	Facts at fingertips about products and services Fast talking, charm; pretend-interest in the buyer; fake matching to their style	Super-keen observation; ability to create rapport Self-possession, genuine interest in the buyer; flexibility; ability to listen
	Haggling and negotiating	Facilitative questioning
Attitudes	Thrill of the chase; hunter; every sale another scalp It's a tough old world, success is scarce; someone has to win and someone has to lose	Partner: a quest for mutual satisfaction Success is possible for both sides. Win–win is the best outcome
Satisfaction	Winning; beating other salespeople	Creating a happy buyer through service
Success rate	Low ratio of success to effort, but hey, it's a game where persistence pays off	High ratio of success to effort. Sales cycle shortened

I believe that the case for this approach as a way of selling coaching is un-assailable. It matches coaching values. It matches coaching skills. It works. If you use it you will make dramatically more sales and reduce the time it takes clients to make up their minds. What more could we ask?

The Buying Facilitation Funnels

Sharon Drew Morgen has a useful model to explain the processes of making a sale.

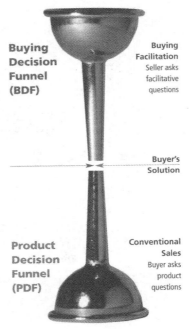

Buying Decision Funnel (BDF)

Buying Facilitation
Seller asks facilitative questions

Buyer's Solution

Product Decision Funnel (PDF)

Conventional Sales
Buyer asks product questions

   The upper funnel is called the Buying Decision Funnel (BDF). This is where the seller asks facilitative questions and the buyer responds. The role of the seller at this point is to act as the coach to the buyer on what he or she wants to buy and all the ramifications that a buying decision will involve. The seller's role is service to the buyer and the emphasis is on the relationship. The pinch point in the middle is reached when it is clear what solution the buyer needs.

   The lower funnel is called the Product Decision Funnel (PDF). Here the roles are reversed. The buyer asks the questions – for instance about costs, features, benefits, and the seller responds. The weakness of conventional sales approaches is that they concentrate only on the PDF. The emphasis in the PDF is on the task of selling and focuses on information.

How it works in practice: selling to individuals

A potential client calls you to say that she'd like to talk to you because she's looking for a coach and has two or three names, all recommended by colleagues or friends. You may hear this process called a variety of things: the *Look–See*, the *Chemistry Meeting*, the *Trial Run* – and so on.

Preparation: service, not selling

As a beginner coach I used to feel a mixture of anxiety and exhilaration when these requests came in. The feeling that I had to perform was often uppermost and pressure to perform (i.e. be something that you are not) inevitably leads to performance anxiety. Two things can happen. First, ego gets in the way and the client detects an unattractive swagger in how you put yourself across. There's too much about you in the conversation. I have often noted a tendency to retreat into the safety zone of coaching jargon when I am in this frame of mind because I'm serving my needs, not the client's. The second possibility is that anxiety suffuses you: *Am I good enough? This is a very important and senior person. They probably already know more than I do. How on earth can I help them?* The result can be either too much nervous and self-effacing chatter or the mental paralysis which means that you dry up.

It is much better to approach these meetings with calm curiosity and pleasant anticipation. You are relaxed but alert. You have reminded yourself of what you already know of this client – probably not much, but that is immaterial at this stage. You have set ego aside. Your role is to serve the client in her quest for a coach. Finding out the answer to the question of whether you can work fruitfully together is a joint enterprise. She may or may not be the right client for me. She may or may not need coaching and, if she does, you may or may not be the person who can provide it. It depends on what she needs. Your purpose is to establish what this is. Believe me, knowing that this is your role is hugely invigorating. It releases you from anxiety and therefore you will be authentic. Not least, it will also give the client a reliable flavour of what it would be like working with you as a coach.

There are a few other points that it is worth bearing in mind. First, this is a buying and selling meeting, not a coaching meeting. Don't be tempted to start coaching. For this reason, keep it short. Forty minutes is plenty and thirty minutes is often enough. It is easier for both you and the client to do the whole thing on the telephone unless the client specifically asks to meet face to face.

Finally, accept that your responsibility is to provide the process framework for the conversation, just as it is in coaching. If you give this responsibility to the buyer, she will flounder and so will you. When this happens, the most likely consequences are:

An uneasy conversation that see-saws confusingly between pleasant general chat and selling.

A philosophical discussion about coaching.

Demands from the buyer that you go straight into selling mode – *So go on – show me what you offer!*

None of these approaches has a high chance of achieving a sale.

A facilitative questions template

These questions have proved their value many times over for me and for my colleagues. Notice their content-free nature. That will keep you out of the ever-present temptation to ask for more facts and details than you need. Customize them to your own vocabulary and style, but stick to the principles while you are learning this process. The questions cut to the heart of what the client needs – remember that is the main purpose of the meeting.

The questions

[If on the phone] *Hullo is that X? Is now a good time for us to have the conversation about coaching? It will take us about 25 minutes.* [If face to face, re-confirm the time you expect the meeting to last; offer coffee, tea or water.]

> Check how the potential client likes to be addressed. There is nothing worse than having your name mispronounced, or to be addressed by a nickname only used by close friends. Checking or rechecking whether the client has the time to talk indicates respect for a busy person's time and is frank about the need for a thorough mutual review. If the answer is no, fix a time to make the call.

It would help us both to hear a bit about the background, why you want a coach and what you want to achieve with coaching. Is it OK if we spend fifteen minutes or so with me asking you some questions? The purpose is to help us both establish what you want and whether or not I'm the right person for you.

> Alerts the client to your role in guiding the first part of the conversation and is frank about purpose and about the amount of time it will take. It is also clear that the process of choosing a coach is matched by the process of choosing a client. This startles clients who are much more used to the frantic sales pitches of the conventional sales process and it also sets expectations for what is to come.

I believe you're in XYZ job/role. Could you tell me a bit about what that involves?

> The initial rapport-creating stage. Executive coaching clients often have awe-inspiringly large responsibilities and conspicuously successful careers. Use your response to this question to acknowledge this – there will be plenty in the client's life that is working well and this gives them the opportunity to tell you what that is.

That sounds as if it's all going pretty well. So what's triggered the feeling that you could benefit from having a coach?

> This is the equivalent of the *why now?* question that you will often ask when working on a specific issue with a client. The answer is always interesting and relevant – often an immediate crisis which masks some underlying and more important concern.

How well were things going along before that?

> This question asks the client to tap into a broader picture and often starts the process of getting to the underlying issues. From your perspective as the coach you will be beginning to see how and why they need a coach because something will be missing. Your role is to identify what that missing piece is.

Summarize so far: *So what I'm hearing is . . . . is that right?*

> This shows the client that you have been listening. You can only do this accurately and skilfully if you have been listening and are in rapport.

What have you already tried in the way of dealing with these issues?

> People will virtually always have considered cheaper or easier options than coming to a coach. For instance, they may have consulted their internal HR person, bought a self-help book or consulted family and friends. On the rare occasions when they haven't, it may be worth diverting to encourage the client to consider what cheaper and easier options there might be. Why would you want to coach someone if they could get what they need at a fraction of the cost in time and money somewhere else?

What's your own feeling about what needs to change?

> This gives the prospective client a strong hint that in order to change others, they have to be willing to change themselves. A wise client is the one who goes thoughtfully silent at this point and begins to sketch out exactly what she sees your joint curriculum as being.

What would need to be different in terms of your own beliefs about all these issues for the coaching to work?

This is an optional question, but for the actual coaching to work, the client's beliefs and assumptions about familiar problems will most probably have to change – especially their assumptions about what they can and can't do. Sometimes, the answer to this question will be a candid, *I'd have to believe I was capable of changing!*

What's at stake for you if nothing changes?

This gives the prospective client the chance to review the cost of staying the same. If it is low then it will not be worth doing the coaching. If it's high – and it usually is – then this probably reinforces the client's emerging decision that coaching is the right solution, if it is.

Summarize again

Shows the client you're still on track and listening hard.

So if the coaching you're looking for went really well, what would be different for you?

As in coaching itself, this question draws on the client's resourcefulness and implies that solutions are indeed possible. It also gives you both vital information about what the client expects.

Who else needs to be involved in the decision to take on a coach?

The systems perspective is often important. There may be a gatekeeper or some other go-between. The budget-holder may be someone different from the potential client. Some organizations insist on clients talking to at least three possible coaches. There may be a life or business partner who could block progress. There may be a budgetary limitation. If so, you need to know.

Have you had a coach before – or a counsellor or mentor? [Then, depending on the answer] *How did that go?*

This gives you vital information. Our buying patterns tend to be the same each time. Knowing what your prospective client's buying pattern is will help both of you see how well you fit with what they need.

Which/how many other coaches are you considering?

The answer may often be *none*. Where clients are scouting the market, they may be willing to tell you who your competitors are. If so, this gives you useful information about their buying criteria. I will sometimes offer to suggest a few names if the client seems to be able to benefit from it. I will also draw attention to the other coaches in our own company, all of whom have biogs on our website and will suggest that the client looks at those, even if only briefly, if they have not already done so.

What was it that put me on your shortlist?

It's always useful to know why potential clients thought you might be a good fit with what they need and who has recommended them. Also it is a good double check on your marketing plan to find out how clients have made their way to you.

What are you looking for in a coach? [Then as a follow-up, depending on the answers] *Which of those is the most and least important for you?*

This question is about the client's criteria. You may or may not fit them.

Summarize the whole conversation. You are now at the end of the buying-decision phase.

Ask: *So where do we go from here?*

It is important to say *we*. You are enclosing the client in a joint process of decision.

The client may say

Thank you very much, I need to go away and think about it.

Or

Send me a proposal/brochure.

If this happens, view it with a sinking heart. If you are a poor match to what the client needs, you should already have said so and brought the meeting to an early close. Mostly, these comments from clients are ways of buying time and there will be something about the conversation that you have not handled well. The exceptions are those occasions where you have already established that the client needs to square the purchase with a third party. In this case, if there is a request for a proposal, follow it up by asking what, specifically, he or she would like included in it, how it should be presented and to what deadline. A much more likely response at this stage is: *I have some questions for you!* Good. You are now in the selling phase of the lower funnel (PDF) and this is where the client asks the questions and you give the product information answers. If the client does not spontaneously ask to get into question-mode, encourage her to do so. These questions will generally take three forms:

- *Information* from you about how far you match the client's criteria on choosing a coach – for instance, if the client has stated that knowledge of her sector is important, then show her that you have it. If you are not a good match on something that the client has said is important to her, then say so and invite the client to review how much that criterion actually matters.
- *Agreement* about what the coaching will involve in terms of effort on both sides: accountability, 'homework', commitment to dates and the hard work that coaching involves. As a coach you will already know that people will only change when they believe they can cope with the turbulence that follows – in the case of coaching, changes to cherished beliefs, giving up dysfunctional behaviours and learning new ones, and so on.
- *Mechanics:* length of sessions, fees, how many sessions, gaps between sessions, psychometric questionnaires or 360 reviews, invoicing, back-up services such as email support and any other information that meets the client's criteria.

I find that when the first part of the conversation has proceeded much as above, the selling stage is remarkably short – perhaps only five minutes because by then the client is getting out her diary and we are already arranging the first session.

Follow up the same day with an email or a letter summarizing the agreement on numbers of sessions, fees, first date and location, adding some form of personal message indicating how much you are looking forward to starting the work. Note: if you are not looking forward to it, then this is not the client for you.

What if?

What if you feel you can't work with the client?

What you do depends on the cause of your unease.

A potential client who is stuck in victim mode is one that every coach dreads. People who constantly blame others cannot face the pain of realizing that they themselves are at least part of the problem. Their fear of being responsible for themselves is overwhelming and they find the idea terrifying that to change others they will have to change themselves. This tendency will surface at the selling meeting. Explain that coaching is about change and surface your doubts about whether you are the right coach for this client. Once gently but straightforwardly challenged in this way, the client will more than likely have decided against you anyway and you can end the meeting on cordial terms.

Other occasions when you might think twice or more about taking on a client might be:

The client is a friend or family member – this should be a coaching-free zone.

The client is unclear about why he wants coaching and remains vague even after you have done your best to clarify it with him.

The client has been recommended by a third party who wants him to have the coaching more than he wants to have it. This could change, but assess it at the selling meeting.

The client has troubling psychological problems which are beyond your skills.

The client has a totally transactional outcome in mind. An example would be a potential client whose organization is willing to pay for coaching on the understanding that it will result in a personal development plan which will be scrutinized and then decreed a pass/fail. I will not do work on these terms as it runs counter to all my values as a coach.

The client's organization wants reports on the client. Explain that coaching is a different process from assessment and if they persist, refuse the assignment courteously while expressing a continuing wish to work with them to do coaching as you understand it, if and when they need it or to undertake assessment under different 'rules' and processes.

What if the client demands that you sell yourself, traditional style?

Refuse. Get a grip on the process framework of the conversation – remember it's your responsibility. Clients behave like this when you have not established control over this part of the conversation and they do it out of unease. They don't know the rules of the game. You do. Ask politely for some time to establish what he needs, explaining that this will pay off for both of you. If that fails, ask what outstanding questions the client has and give brief responses before asking for his consent to revert to the facilitative questions.

What if you sense that something has gone wrong somewhere in the process?

If your rapport skills are everything they need to be, you will know when this has happened. You will feel the client withdrawing. Signs that he is doing this will be the unmistakable cues of someone getting ready to end the conversation: not responding to your questions fully, avoiding eye contact, tidying his papers, fiddling with a briefcase, folding up his glasses. The cause will virtually always be that you have entered the selling phase of the conversation too soon. Instead of ignoring it, draw attention to it. It may not be too late to retrieve the situation. Say: *I sense that I'm going off track a bit here. Have I said or done something that's hit a wrong note for you?*

Honesty and genuineness may save the day. As I walked away from what I already knew full well was a failed opportunity to sell a coaching programme to an interesting client whom I had liked, I realized that my antennae had not been well enough tuned during the meeting to pick up his clear signals that I was talking too much. Later, with rueful hindsight I realized that I had jumped far too quickly from establishing his criteria to showing him how amply I could meet them, without summarizing, pausing or truly bottoming out his needs. If I had been less cocky and less concerned with impressing, I might have noticed this properly at the time and drawn back from the pit I had dug for myself.

What if the client asks your opinion of competitors?

You handle this openly and respectfully. Never criticize the opposition. A sensible client will have done a market scan anyway. The more you know about this, the better equipped you are to understand what the client's decision-making processes are. Remember you are working to his or her buying patterns, not yours.

> *Jules Boardman*
> Jules was looking for a coaching course having had a successful career as an entrepreneur. He had sold his company and was ready to make a complete career switch to coaching as long as he could be sure that he was suited to it. He rang me to discuss our course. He told me straight away that he had spent several weeks on market research and was finding the coach-training market 'incredibly confusing with so many websites all seeming to say the same things'. What I said to Jules was:
>
> > I don't want anyone to come on our course who is not right for it – in the sense that it would not meet their needs. I'd rather they bought elsewhere.
> >
> > He sounded an intriguing potential coach but part of the purpose of the course was for people to find out if they were as suited to coaching as they believed.
> >
> > It's the beginning of a long process of learning, not a once and for all qualification.

I know our competitors and what they offer through and through. I like many of them – would Jules like to hear my take on the market?

Yes, he would. I emphasized that he would not be hearing all this from a neutral party so it would be important for him to check it out for himself and that I would give him contact details later in the conversation. I then gave him a summary account of how I saw the main coach-training providers.

We had established his criteria early in the conversation and I knew that we were an excellent match to what he said he wanted. However, I encouraged him to ring the three competitors whom I rate and to have the same conversation with them that he had had with me.

In calling to say that he was accepting the offer of a place, Jules said that my 'friendly and fair' description of competitors was what had made him decide to buy from us. *I learnt more from you in twenty minutes than I had from weeks browsing the Internet . . .* and then as a smiling afterthought, *Where did you learn to sell like that?*

Jules is now well on track with his own coaching business, concentrating on executives in the arts, entertainment, sport and advertising industries, all of which he knows from first-hand experience (jules@jbecm.com).

Ideas to consider for a more developed business

In the early stages of developing a coaching business, it will feel enough to obtain individual clients. But as your business grows, you will become more ambitious. You will be looking for bigger contracts.

Selling to organizations

Although it may feel more daunting to sell to an organization, in fact the core of the process is recognizably the same. In the end it comes down to selling a relationship through service, whether it's a contract to an individual coach to work with all the members of a small team, or to a company to supply coaching over a longer period to several hundred of its staff.

The difference is that the systems perspective is always more complex in organizations. Accept that just as you will never know all the ins and outs of a client's personal life, you can never understand the complexities of decision-making in an organization unless you are part of it and even then you will not see the whole picture. This is why there is so often a mysterious time-lag between making the pitch and hearing whether your client is going to buy (i.e. this is the length of the sales cycle). It is so easy to be misled into thinking that you are talking to the decision-maker when actually there is a complex web of alliances and egos behind the scenes. Organizations are systems and systems resist change – they will always try to preserve equilibrium, for instance by correcting whatever appears to be wrong with a short-term fix to the presenting symptom. (For more on this and the typical archetypes that recur constantly in organizations and elsewhere, see Peter Senge's classic book, *The Fifth Discipline*.)

So when you sell to an organization you will know a lot less than everyone inside it about:

its culture;

its buying norms;

the complexities of the turf wars;

who has the real power and who is only a pretender;

how the organization will handle the upheaval that change involves.

All this has to be taken into account in your questioning.

Example

A colleague was rung by a pleasant-sounding young man who introduced himself as the Organization Development Facilitator for his organization. He was interested in buying coaching and 'group support' for up to one hundred staff whose jobs were at risk in a coming NHS reorganization.

> *Trap 1*: assuming that because we have delivered this kind of package many times in the past for the NHS, the same kind of support would be needed here.
> *Trap 2*: assuming that we knew what 'group support' meant.
> *Trap 3*: assuming that we were talking to the decision-maker.

As the colleague began to use the facilitative questions format, she concentrated especially on the systems aspect. This revealed the complexities behind the apparent simplicity of the first enquiry. Our contact actually worked for a consortium of organizations and was the professional coordinator for the project. He reported to a sub-committee of a committee of Chief Executives over an entire region. He was the only member of this committee with any understanding of the quality issues involved in coaching as he had done a coaching qualification himself. This sub-committee was controlled by a Health Authority with a powerful Chief Executive. Much manoeuvring behind the scenes was involved in deciding what to do about staff whose jobs were at risk. The at-risk list included several of those on the sub-committee.

My colleague's role in this conversation? To establish what the buying criteria were and then what kind of next step the contact needed from us. Our contact thanked my colleague warmly for helping him clarify the decision-making process, told her that he now realized that he needed to establish his own authority as the only person in this group with professional knowledge of coaching, and in response to *What's the next step for us here?* asked for *a piece of paper outlining what you could offer.*

What kind of piece of paper?

An email, A4 one-side equivalent, just summarizing what we've discussed and setting out what you could do so that I can use it as a prompt at the next meeting. If you could get it to me by tomorrow that would be great. I don't need a formal proposal.

Would you need referees included?

No – they already know people who've used your services; that's why you're one of the people I'm contacting.

In this case the sales cycle was only a week. The conversation recounted above had significantly changed the buyer's mental landscape and he told us later that we were the only company of the three he contacted that had bothered to, as he put it, *get behind the façade.*

The ideal: how it could work in practice

Stage 1: The contact
You meet an acquaintance at a networking event who tells you that his organization is looking for coaches. Probably only the senior members of one team are likely to be involved at this stage, but you're a coach: would you be interested?

Of course you are. You ask him whom to contact and he is a little vague – he thinks it might be X. This is not at all unusual. The information about the need could be reliable but your contact does not know for certain who the decision-maker is, so that is your next step. You ask him if you may mention his name when you ring X; he agrees readily and you thank your contact heartily, promising to let him know what happens. In fact, cherish this contact because he will be one of those people who enjoys connecting one person to another (see page 76).

Stage 2: The PA is your ally

Every PA I have ever worked with has seen it as her job to screen out un-wanted callers but also – often forgotten – to let in those who could be useful. All have had gruesome tales of the rudeness of callers who assume that she is an inferior being. All have been experts in the informal systems in the organization because bosses talk unguardedly to their PAs and PAs talk to other PAs.

So on your call to X's office the next day, you will be treating the PA in the same way that you will be treating X – using rapport skills, the same facilitative questions and the same holding-off from brash selling.

- Introduce yourself and mention that your contact of the previous day has suggested that you ring. Ask her name: *Who am I talking to?* Ask if she has time to talk to you. If not, agree a time to ring back.
- Say frankly that you are interested in offering coaching to the organization, so that she knows that you are making a sales call. Don't disguise it because it will be obvious anyway.
- Ask her name and role. Write it down and put it into your address system because you will need it later.
- Ask her what she knows about how the organization is handling the need for coaching.
- Seek her help in identifying who the decision-maker is. It may or may not be X. If it is, ask when it would be a good time to call him or her. Fix the time there and then.

As Sharon Drew Morgan comments, remember that *anyone* who answers the phone is your client.

Stage 3: Talking to the decision-maker

Use the facilitative questions template (page 90) just as you would in a one-to-one conversation, remembering to concentrate especially on the systems aspects. Make it clear at the outset that you are making a sales call. This is so refreshing when compared to the inappropriate scripted nonsense of the usual cold call.

When you get to the *Where do we go from here?* question, the likely an-swers might include:

setting up a face-to-face meeting to meet other decision-makers;

a brief email or letter summing up what you offer, concentrating, of course, only on the aspects which the client is interested in buying;

setting up a session immediately for X as your first client;

introductions to other possible coaching clients.

Handling the contact in this way shortens the sales cycle, reduces the need for elaborate proposals (many of which turn out to be wide of the mark when not preceded by the facilitative process) and builds foundations for a long-term relationship where both sides benefit.

What if they already have a supplier?
Never put down the existing supplier or seek to supplant them, but you will not know how happy the organization is with them. Ask, *Are there any circumstances in which you'd consider adding another supplier to your list of coaches?*

What if I'm too expensive?
It's better to establish this during the first contact than later. If people are buying on price, and some people do, then it is inevitable that you will be too expensive for some and too cheap for others. If your prices are within 10 per cent of what the organization considers fair, then you could express willingness to discount if everything else has gone well in the conversation. Alternatively, you could offer an introductory round of coaching as a pilot, making it clear that depending on the outcome, you would wish to revert to your normal fee pattern later.

Tenders

This is one of the main ways in which larger contracts are obtained. Tenders are an awkward fact of life for coaches. Their purpose is positive: to safeguard the organization from corruption and to keep costs competitive by establishing a transparent process which could withstand public scrutiny. Made apparently essential by a number of well-publicized local government scandals in the 1960s and 1970s, they have now spread everywhere in the public sector and to many parts of the private sector as well.

The market trend is that organizations have become more interested in coaching as an effective development process for their most senior staff. Discovering that many of these staff were being enterprising enough to buy for themselves eventually created alarm: *Who are these coach people? How do we know they are any good? What's it costing? What do we get out of it – how will we know it's working? How consistent is the coaching in its approach? Shouldn't we control and regulate?* These are good questions. This is why organizations interested in coaching, as virtually all large organizations now are, will try either to establish an agreed list of suppliers who have passed quality hurdles, or to put a single contract out to tender.

The main disadvantage of tenders when you are the vendor is that they put you in the position of having to sell without the opportunity to facilitate the buying decision. This is why the chances of success are so small as it then becomes hit or miss whether what you offer fits what the buyer really needs.

I have been on both sides of this fence. In my earlier career I was a Commissioning Editor and part of my job was letting large contracts for TV and print, some of it funded by government money. What I discovered there was what a time-consuming hassle the whole tendering process is for the person letting the contract as well as for the person who competes for it. I found out how often you end up with the person you first thought of because the relationship is already one of mutual respect. I also realized that when you sat down thoughtfully and wrote a proper specification, it was usually obvious whom you needed to approach.

The cost of tenders in disappointment and anxiety on both sides is high and the cost in time and money is astronomical. Courtesy can often get overlooked. Our worst experience here was competing for some work with an ambulance organization who asked for a detailed proposal, invited us to a beauty parade which took a whole day of two people's time and then never contacted us about the result, resolutely ignoring phone calls, letters and emails. At the time we could only hope that they dispatched their ambulances with more politeness and efficiency, which seemed dubious. The most laughable request to bid was being asked if I wanted to compete for *two hours* of work, including submitting a formal proposal. (I suggested someone else.) You will gather from this that I am sceptical about whether tendering does actually deliver the payback it promises to *clients* for the time and money it costs.

However, the public sector is massive in the UK and is probably the biggest single market for coaching. If this is now how clients want to appoint coaches then we must accept that this is their privilege. It is worth competing for bigger contracts because it guarantees a flow of work and also gives you the chance to get to know a client organization in depth, with all the opportunities for interesting work that this will generate.

Deciding to enter the race

When you are starting off, this whole area may feel as if it is out of your league, but in fact it is easy to create a consortium of like-minded fellow-coaches for purposes of competing for a contract. A trio of my supervision clients did just this and won a large contract at their first attempt.

However, you have to be prepared for a degree of hard, tedious work and also to get familiar with the arcane world of tendering acronyms:

EOI: Expression of Interest

PQQ: Pre-Qualification Questionnaire

RFP: Request for Proposal

ITT: Invitation to Tender

At any stage, but particularly at the PQQ stage, you might be asked for:

> your policies on health, safety, the environment and diversity;

> audited accounts for the last year available, sometimes for the last three years;

> evidence of your Quality Assurance policy;

> confirmation that you have insurance cover;

> CVs (brief biographies, see page 49) of all staff you are putting forward;

> guarantees that principals/directors have not been involved in bankruptcy or criminal activity.

For some companies or government departments you may have to have security clearance.

There may or may not be a number of other rituals surrounding the process. For instance, the bid usually has to be placed inside the supplied envelope and delivered by a stated time on the stated day. A little flexibility on the part of the client is welcome here. We were allowed, for instance, to submit our bid three hours late on one occasion because our courier had fallen off his motorbike and was having his leg stitched in A&E when he should have been delivering our package. It may only be possible to submit written questions on the specification and these plus the answers will be solemnly circulated to all bidders. This is a bad sign because it suggests an organization taking itself far too seriously.

Preparing and writing the bid is time-consuming and can be exasperating – not least if you are dealing with a Purchasing Department which knows nothing and cares less about coaching. If you get shortlisted then you have to be prepared to give up at least half a day to attend the beauty parade with theoretically only a one in three to one in six chance of winning. If this has not put you off, then carry on reading.

Finding out what contracts are being let
This is relatively easy. The best route is to be contacted directly by a gatekeeper who already knows you and likes your work. Informal networking will of course also alert you to what is coming up and you can ask your contact to

include you in any invitations. The gatekeeper may be contacting probably no more than three potential suppliers and may make it clear that this contract will not be advertised. Your success rate will be higher when this is the case because it speaks of a thoughtful client who is clued up about what they want.

Failing that, there are two other routes. The trade press in your sector may carry advertisements inviting expressions of interest. Alternatively, it may have editorial copy describing the investment in coaching that a particular organization is planning to make. For government work, there is a magazine, *Contrax Weekly,* also available online, devoted exclusively to advertisements of public sector contracts. You will have to decide whether the cost of subscription is worth what you might get out of it.

Deciding whether to bid

Be choosy about what you bid for and what you let pass by. I know of at least one successful coaching organization whose policy is never to compete for tenders. If they cannot obtain the work, including from government departments, through direct negotiation, they hold back. Their considered view is that the opportunity-cost of preparing tenders is too big to justify the small chances of winning. We have taken the opposite view and a huge percentage of our own work now comes this way, but we are selective. Here are some guidelines about how to choose which tender to go for and which to let go:

Bad signs	Good signs
The specification is vague	There is a detailed specification clearly written by someone who knows what coaching is
What they seem to want overlaps to some extent with what you can offer, but not fully	The specification is a close match to what you can offer
The ITT asks for enormous amounts of detail on areas that could only be arrived at through negotiation with the client once you had got the work	The ITT acknowledges that details can be worked out later, in partnership
There are no success criteria	It includes success criteria and how they will be weighted You can match 90 per cent of them
There is no contact name, or if there is, it is someone in the purchasing department	There is a contact name and the contact is a senior coaching or HR professional
The contact can only be reached by email	The contact is willing to talk freely about what he or she wants

Bad signs	Good signs
You have never worked for this organization	The organization is already a client
You are responding out of the blue	You have been invited to tender
You feel discourteously treated in any one-to-one contact	You are treated with respect and friendliness throughout

You may want to pay particular attention to the last point on the list above. A colleague went to a pre-tender meeting where potential bidders were being briefed. The meeting was in Wales. He got up at 5.00 a.m. in order to be there, committing himself to a round trip of 500 miles in a 12-hour day. At the meeting, he reported hostile comments directed at *our* English *friend who has* deigned *to be here, and, Of course, it would be difficult for anyone English to understand the situation here in Wales.* Some of the meeting was conducted in Welsh, without translation, in spite of the high probability that the number of Welsh speakers present was minute. We did not bid for that work. How you are treated during the bidding process is a reliable guide to what it would be like to work with that client. I have never known an exception to this rule.

Increasing your chances of success

Research the organization through the internet. Look at its website and the Annual Report. Assess what message the organization is trying to give through how it presents itself. Look at what has been left out. Contact anyone you know who works there and ask for a briefing.

Where there is a contact name, it always pays to call them. Even when there is an exemplary specification it will be worth using the facilitative questions template as this will reliably generate useful data. The area of success criterion is the one that is most often missing and this is the very area that will be of most value to you in writing your bid.

Ask your contact what style and length of proposal will be most useful and stick to whatever guidelines are suggested.

Proposal format
Concentrate on setting out first how closely your offer matches what the client wants. A useful format of headings is:

A brief summary of what you know about the background and the commissioner's reasons for needing the work – as long as this is not simply parroting back what is in the specification.

Our offer: step by step matching to the specification. This should be the biggest single chunk of the proposal.

Track record: other clients for whom you have done similar work, and referees, if requested.

Staff CVs.

Costs.

Terms and conditions, if not included in the tender papers.

When you have written your first draft, go back to the specification and rigorously check off what it has requested against what you have written. Normally it is best to keep a proposal short and to put any detail into an Appendix. But be guided by your client-contact here.

The beauty parade

Sometimes clients will go straight to this phase. When they do, your chances of success are usually high because they will already have checked you out and you may already have had a buying conversation with them to which this meeting is the response.

Where there is a more formal tendering process, you have made it to the shortlist. In either case, it will pay dividends to prepare carefully:

- Call your contact again and thank her for the chance to show what you can do. Ask her advice about how to play your presentation. Ask who will be present and what their jobs are. Confirm the amount of time you have been given and ask what equipment will be available, if you want to use slides or other visual aids.
- Ask about the dress code, if you don't already know.
- Consider whether to go alone or to take a colleague. Having a companion is usually a better bet – you will feel more supported and it will give the panel a chance to hear two voices and two different ways of operating from the same set of values. It also demonstrates respect for the client by showing that you have taken the invitation seriously.

I prefer to avoid PowerPoint as I think it detracts from the relationship aspect of the occasion. If it is merely a summary of what is already in your bid, what is the purpose? Most judging panels will expect you to launch straight into your presentation – i.e. into selling mode immediately. We have found that in practice, most panels are happy to conduct the whole interview as a conversation. This may seem odd, but hearing the answers to these questions from a group is very different from hearing them from an individual or reading them in a document. Because the custom is to create a space at the start for the pitch, it is usually fine to dispense with it and to create a conversation instead.

Start by asking if this is OK with the panel:

> *We'd like to start by asking you some more questions as a way of us all checking out what kind of fit there is between what we offer and what you need. Is that OK?*

If it is not OK and it is clear that the panel has a rigid process (in itself a bad sign) then start your pitch but pause frequently and invite questions and comments. An example would be:

> *So this is our understanding of what you seem to need, but we'd be interested in hearing what additional information you think we would need to have here.* Then make sure you pause and wait for comment.

However, mostly a panel will agree readily to a request to have a conversation. This gives you some immediate control over the occasion and also emphasizes your wish to service the buying decision rather than to sell.

Then use the questioning template. Once you have got to their criteria, and summed up, offer your pitch, developing it on the spot to match those criteria. We have also found that it helps clients to see immediately what your approach would be if you do some coaching there and then, either with your colleague as a demonstration, or with a willing volunteer from the panel. You have to be very confident of your coaching skills to do this, but if you are not, you would probably not have got this far anyway.

Beware of making direct or implied criticisms of the organization, even if they solicit them. You will never know enough at this stage to be certain that your judgement is right and the chances of causing offence are high. This will later be conveyed to you through feedback as *you didn't really seem to understand our problems thoroughly enough.*

When it is all over and the clients have made their decision, always ask for feedback whatever the outcome. When you have been chosen, ask:

> *What specifically did we write, say or do that convinced you we were the right people for you?*

If you have been beaten by a competitor, ask:

> *What specifically could we do another time to impress you more?*
> *What other opportunities could there be for us to work with you?*
> *What should we do to follow them up?*

Regard all these events, however they turn out, as opportunities to build the relationship and to hone your selling skills. We have frequently found that when we have not been successful with a bid, by asking these follow-up questions we have been offered other work which in due course has led to the kind of bigger contract we were seeking in the first place.

Absolute essentials

- Accept that learning how to sell – and confronting your fears about it – is fundamental to the success of your business.
- Concentrate first on selling one-to-one through the *look–see*: success here will increase your confidence.
- Learn the *facilitative questions* template and adapt it to your own style.

---

6 Up and Running: Managing Your Brand

Let's suppose your business is now up and running. You have a developing client base. You are working with a couple of associates now and again. You are beginning to think about bidding for bigger contracts. By doing this you will have developed, perhaps in just fledgling stage, a *brand* which has value and which must be shaped and protected. You can't leave this vital task to chance. This chapter is about how to do it. It concerns your values, purpose, ethics and customer-service policy and how these influence your business success. The sum total is your brand: the ultimate and elusive reason why clients will choose you rather than a competitor.

Values and why they matter

Conscious awareness of what your values are will have a number of advantages for your business. It will define how people experience working with you because it will permeate every exchange with clients. I am asked surprisingly often why I am in coaching and what I get from it. This question is not about what income I make. It is a question about values and purpose, so it helps to have an answer ready. (Note that this is a different question from 'What do you do?' – page 60.)

Knowing what your values are will make difficult decisions easier. It will increase the satisfaction you feel about the work and it is strongly linked with commercial success. Ultimately what you are selling is your reputation and a good reputation has cash value. Clients talk to each other either to recommend you or to check you out. If there is the slightest suspicion that your behaviour is anything but impeccably ethical, no amount of skilful marketing can retrieve what you have lost.

Those of you who work as organization consultants will probably have worked with clients on their Values. It always has a capital V, to signify its importance. Unless painstakingly done, most top teams in organizations will cheerfully and swiftly produce a list something like this:

Our values

Openness

Honesty

Quality

Professionalism

Efficiency

Bla bla

These words trip off the tongue so readily. Linguistically they fall into the category known as *nominalizations* – that is, they are abstract words that can be interpreted however you like. They are utterly meaningless unless they start from deeply held ideological beliefs translated into action and then used as daily decision-making tools. This is far from how they are actually originated and used in many organizations. Much more typically, once the Board has signed off the Values, its members can give a sigh of relief. The list can appear in the Annual Report and then everyone can forget all about it.

Making and then publishing your values list – which I urge you to do – is a high-risk activity. If what people experience is adrift from what you claim then you are in more trouble than if you had never made such a list in the first place. The ultimate example here is the US company, Enron. In 2000, Enron stood as the seventh biggest company in the US. Its growth had been spectacular. The Enron Annual Report listed two, among others, of the company's values:

> *Integrity*
> We treat others as we would like to be treated ourselves. We do not tolerate abusive or disrespectful behaviour.

> *Excellence*
> We are satisfied with nothing less than the very best in everything we do . . . The great fun here will be for all of us to discover just how good we can really be.

By December 2001, the firm had collapsed in a fatal scandal, pursued relentlessly by furious investors, pensioners, regulators and ultimately by the courts. Few of its top executives escaped opprobrium and personal ruin. The case also pulled down its auditors, Arthur Andersen, until then one of the world's most powerful accountancy companies. Enron's leaders had lied grossly about its profits, concealing debts so that they would not appear on its balance sheet. Its corporate culture stood revealed as one of personal greed, cynicism, deceit and swagger: cut-throat cowboy capitalism at its worst. How they must have laughed when they drew up the values list.

What has this got to do with coaching and your coaching business? Everything. The Enron case is not a reason to avoid developing a values list, but it does serve as a warning about how pointless it is unless it starts from authenticity and is translated into action. Every business needs to have ethical guidelines – how the values are interpreted in practice – and to know how to use them.

Values are not a nice-to-have add-on invented by the PR department, as Enron clearly thought. Rather they are part of the pragmatic idealism which is a feature of all profitable organizations. In James Collins's and Jim Porras's thoughtful book *Built to Last,* they identify the features of companies that consistently outperformed their competitors over a long period of time. The research paired companies in the same sectors or business and looked for what distinguished the outstanding (what they call the *visionary*) companies from the merely good of the competitor in the pair:

> Our research showed that a fundamental element in the . . . visionary company is a core ideology – core values and sense of purpose beyond just making money – that guides and inspires people throughout the organizations and remains relatively fixed for long periods of time.

> A detailed pair by pair analysis showed that the visionary companies have generally been more ideologically driven and less purely profit driven than the comparison companies in seventeen out of eighteen pairs. This is one of the clearest differences we found between the visionary and comparison companies.

> (page 55)

In the successful organizations of the Collins and Porras study, all the companies indoctrinate (there's no other word for it) employees into what these values mean in practice. No company in the study had more than six core values. This is not surprising because we are talking here about fiercely held fundamental beliefs, which Collins and Porras describe as being characterized by their *piercing simplicity*.

Purpose

Underneath the values is an even deeper concept: *purpose.* As Collins and Porras's book shows, all successful companies are likely to have a reason for existence which goes beyond just making money. They are in their chosen business because they believe it has something that contributes to the common good. So Disney's core purpose is *bringing happiness to millions*. The BBC has always believed that its purpose is *to inform, educate and entertain* and although the way these words have been interpreted has varied and been fiercely disputed over the eight decades of the Corporation's history, all BBC employees understand to their boots why they matter. These are purposes that can never be outgrown – they are likely to last and are a great deal more motivating for all concerned than a dull description of the company's activities, product lines and services ever could be.

Both you and your clients need to know what your purpose and values are. Making them explicit is part of your offer to your market and also part of how your clients will experience you.

Identifying purpose and mission

Ask yourself these questions:

What drew you to coaching as a profession?

When it is clear that your coaching works, what is the nature of the satisfaction you experience?

What would be missing from your life if you had no opportunities to coach?

The most compelling answers to these questions will be nothing to do with financial reward or the freedom and autonomy that coaching gives you, important though these are. True purpose will be about how coaching meets some deeper need in you about what you offer to the world rather than what you want to take from it. That is why the word *mission* with its deliberately spiritual overtones is so often used as a synonym for *purpose*.

I asked two of my co-Directors at Management Futures, Jan Campbell Young and Phil Hayes, how they answered these questions.

> *Jan*
> Endless curiosity about what makes people tick combined with trusting my intuition. Every situation, every client is different, but underlying them all for me is the great joy you get when they make the changes they want and need. Two of my clients have had babies this week and it was a goal both had set for themselves early in our coaching. I've just this minute had the emailed picture of one of the babies. Fabulous! That's what makes it worth while.

> *Phil*
> I started my career as a social worker and the entire profession was then focused on *problems*. If you like, it was a Freudian view – overcoming your oppression and early disasters with all the

miserablist implications that follow from that mindset. I see coaching as being more Jungian in its inspiration – about achieving your potential and becoming the person you were destined to be. When I discovered NLP and I realized you could work from outcomes not from problems it was fantastically liberating. Coaching is the most powerful thing I've ever come across because it clears the way for outcomes – and knowing what outcome you want makes it so much more likely that you will get it.

Although the actual words may vary, I've yet to hear a successful coach fail to define their core purpose in similar terms. It is always about being of service to others.

Defining your values

Imagine it's five years into the future. Your coaching business is thriving. You are happy and fulfilled.

> Take a moment to set the scene in your mind: what would the other evidence of success be? Write it down here

Now think about your 'stakeholders' – that is anyone whose opinion you value and who can affect the health of your business. What would they be saying about you and your work? How would they describe the behaviour they had experienced?

Examples of stakeholders might be:

> The clients who return again and again/ refer others to you
>
> 'Gatekeeper' clients – the people who refer clients to you
>
> Suppliers – for instance, the professional advisers who work with you (accountant, bookkeeper, lawyer)

> Any support staff which by then you might have – e.g. a PA
>
> Associates
>
> Important people in your personal life

Take them one by one and write down in the boxes above what you imagine they would say about the experience of working with you. What under-pinning values does this exercise reveal? Look for between four and six.

This is just the start. As the Enron experience shows, the words are meaningless until they are translated into behaviour. One way to do this is to ask yourself what positive behaviour people would observe and what its negative opposite would also be.

Here are two examples of how it might look:

Value	Positive indicators	Negative indicators
Integrity	I am straightforward with clients about what to expect from me and from coaching I turn away anyone who could not benefit from what I offer	I take on anyone who will pay the fee
Efficiency	I return phone calls/answer emails within 24 hours I never cancel sessions for trivial reasons I pay my suppliers promptly	I'm sloppy about messages and phone calls I'm casual about altering appointments I play the field with suppliers – I have to wait for payment, so why shouldn't they?

Values and decision-making

Getting clear about this is a way of making tough decisions. Here is an example. One of our values at Management Futures is *generosity*. How does this feature in our work? The answer is that it helps us a great deal in daily decision-making. Some recent examples would be:

Looking specifically for evidence of generosity as a character trait when we hire people.

Encouraging an employee in his wish to move on, although it was actually against our own short-term interests to do so.

Offering free coaching to a liked and valued client who was temporarily out of work.

Offering electronic copies of handouts to an associate who also works for a competitor.

While all this could make us seem saintly, in fact it is enlightened self-interest. The employee might well return to us at some point in the future as an associate and we wanted to part with him on good terms. The valued client soon got another job and has already recommended us for a large piece of organizational development work. Similarly, we are generous with our handouts as long as people ask permission and keep the copyright acknowledgement because we take the software view that there will be another one along shortly.

It has to be said that our generosity is tempered by our energetic pursuit of new business. We are also prepared to strike hard bargains because we have a proper appreciation of our market value and are tough with ourselves and employees where meeting our quality standards is concerned. However, there is no getting away from the fact that generosity as a core human and business value matters a lot to us. We see ourselves as giving as well as taking and this philosophy has guided us from the outset.

Ethical principles: the link to the bottom line

There are many versions of codes of ethics for coaches. The ethical code we use is quoted in my book, *Coaching Skills: A Handbook* (page 163). This book also contains a discussion of the dilemmas that ethical principles could throw up in your coaching transactions with clients and that is not my topic here. Our code is similar to dozens of others, including the version in development by the EMCC (www.emccouncil.org).

What is not so frequently pointed out is the relevance of ethics to business success.

Clients first

All codes of ethics in the helping professions have this principle at their core. By knowing that you put clients first you will be prepared to act against your own short-term commercial interests. Always be prepared to walk away if you suspect that this principle could be violated. Examples:

A potential client desperate to work with you but whom you feel will not be able to benefit from the work.

You suspect that the organization wants you to coach someone with whom they soon intend to part. The coaching is a fig leaf, designed to show that they did everything possible to 'help' the person.

The client wants a particular slant to the coaching which you are not qualified to deliver.

The commercial benefit of saying no is that clients will respect you. It will go against what is, sadly, becoming one of the standard journalistic ways of referring to coaching – as a profession where greedy people exploit the gullible.

Openness: prevention not cure

The secret is complete candour at the outset and throughout the life of a coaching project. Whether you are negotiating a single coaching programme for an individual client or a big contract with an organization, explore all the ramifications before the deal is signed and sealed. Ask:

What do we expect of each other?

What are the conditions we need for success?

Where could this go wrong?

How could we act now to prevent things going wrong?

How will we review the work as we go?

What do we need to put in writing about our agreement?

Such openness is not just a nice-to-have. There is a commercial cost – for instance, unpaid and energy-sapping meetings, and possibly legal fees as well if major misunderstanding creeps in. The positive benefit is that where there is openness you will increase the possibility many times over of building a long-term and mutually enjoyable relationship.

The duty of care

As a coach you have a duty to uphold the law and to protect individuals, society and the environment from harm. This may seem obvious, but actually committing in practice to such a principle would have saved Enron and Arthur Andersen from the disaster that engulfed them both. An Australian coach once told me how important it was to his coaching and consulting practice to have had this ethical principle made explicit. The practice by chance discovered a way of avoiding tax. It was illegal and there was virtually no prospect of discovery. *If we had cheated here*, he said, *it would have made it seem OK to cheat in other ways. We don't like paying tax any more than anyone else, but it's the law and that is part of our duty of care.* Word got out about this incident. My contact links it explicitly to the award of a big coaching contract from a government department where the gatekeeper client had been one of those in the know and had been duly impressed.

Confidentiality

All coaches sign up to confidentiality – in theory. But perhaps all do not realize the commercial risk of breaching it. Clients judge by what they experience. We recently competed for a coaching contract. The circumstances were unusual. The initial contract with one of our competitors had been terminated before its due end and was to be re-let, purely on grounds that details of client sessions had leaked copiously into the organization.

Fees

I discuss how you set fees on pages 35–41. The ethical dimension is to be scrupulously open and transparent about the process. Good practice is to:

- avoid padding contracts with contingency clauses on which you know you will never need to call;
- contact clients who have unused sessions and ask them what they would like to do – the most likely reply is 'keep them for a rainy day';
- keep prices consistent as far as possible. If you do have differential pricing (for instance between public and private sector work), make the differences clear and upfront;
- be clear with the client about what the coaching includes or excludes. Send confirmation in writing, including what your policy is on cancellations. Be aware that if you enforce a cancellation policy in a draconian way you may lose that client's good will permanently. However, be prepared to be tough with clients who consistently cancel their sessions at short notice. This is disrespectful on their part and you do not have to put up with disrespect;
- remember that clients hate fee surprises. If you are going to charge for extras of any kind (sessions, expenses, materials), negotiate first. Some clients expect to have introductory can-we-work-together meetings and these are always free. Corporate clients will also resist paying fees for whole-project review meetings held at their request.

Anticipate such meetings at the outset and either build them explicitly and openly into your bid or regard them as the price of goodwill.

Avoiding conflicts of interest

Conflicts of interest can pop up in coaching in all kinds of ways. The most common are:

being asked to coach people at similar levels or similar jobs in competitor organizations or departments;

being asked to coach two candidates for the same job;

learning about commercial developments in a client organization which could have share-value implications (be specially wary of this one, as if you act on it, it counts as *insider dealing* and is illegal);

being on the inside track of a client organization through another route – for instance being a non-executive director or through a personal relationship with a senior person who could be in a position to influence the decision to hire you. You may be pure as pure in such cases, but it will be hard to defend the fairness of any contract you win here if challenged publicly;

being entertained by or entertaining a client in ways that might compromise your or their reputation.

When you decide that there is a damaging conflict of interest, either raise it with clients or make the decision to walk away and tell them why. Either tactic will bolster your reputation as an honourable operator, strengthening your chances of winning other work in future. An important principle here is that not only must you behave fairly, you must be seen to be behaving fairly.

Respecting intellectual rights

Respect other people's work. This means:

- Ask permission to copy – it will usually be granted readily.
- Acknowledge copyright and sources – don't pass other people's work off as your own.
- Respect the warning not to copy when it is explicitly forbidden: normally this will be because you can buy legitimate copies cheaply.
- Use only those psychometric instruments in which you have been trained and licensed.

- Where you quote research, quote it accurately either because you have actually read the original work or a reliable digest. Never rely on 50th-hand claims. Distortion and exaggeration is the inevitable consequence. An example would be the often-quoted research into what percentage of communication is conveyed non-verbally. The original modest research project is typically quoted as a gospel truth set of generalizations which 'prove' wildly inflated assertions given as percentages. The name of the research author (Mehrabian) is commonly misspelt. This is not good practice. Every now and again, you could meet a client who knows any research you quote better than you do. This client will for sure let the world know that your expertise is not reliable, even if they avoid embarrassing you at the time.

Business relationships with third parties

You will often be in the situation of referring a client to a third party. This might be to one of the strategic business partners discussed on page 74, or to a specialist dealing in some particular topic which is beyond your own expertise. Where you have a business relationship with the third party, you must disclose it. If you keep it quiet and the client later discovers that this is the case, the client will immediately doubt the impartiality of your recommendation, whereas if you are open about it both you and the client will know where you stand.

Acting promptly on doubts

Where you have doubts about the ethical status of any issue, don't wait for such doubts to go away on their own. If you have doubts, you are probably right to worry. Discuss them with a colleague or supervisor, raise them early with the client and agree on action.

A warning from the front line

If nothing else, let fear of punishment be your guide. A few years ago a coaching client handed me a report from an Assessment Centre in which she had been a candidate. She had been rejected for a public sector job, one of nearly thirty appointments being made simultaneously for very senior and high-profile jobs. As part of her search for a new job, she wanted to make sense of the written feedback she had received at the Assessment Centre. This feedback was based on the output of psychometric tests and observations made at the Centre.

As I read her report, my astonishment and anger grew. I was reading several pages of my own words, illegally copied from my book on the psychometric questionnaire FIRO-B (co-authored with Judy Waterman), a flagrant breach of the ethics by which all users of psychometric materials are bound. The only difference was that where Judy and I had used the word *you*, the Assessment Centre candidate's name had been substituted. Neither we nor the publisher had been asked permission and if we had, this was one of the occasions on which it would have been refused. This book was the outcome of months of diligent work on our part and the culmination of many years of unique joint expertise. Our work had been stolen. These were my options:

1   Expose the culprit to the world, specifically to the publisher/UK distributor, renowned for his feisty attitude to breaches of copyright and who might be prepared to seek redress through the courts.
2   Expose the culprit to the client who had commissioned the Assessment Centre.
3   Complain to the company running the Centre, demanding a grovelling apology to Judy and me, and an appropriate punishment for the consultant concerned.
4   Do nothing.

I ruled out option 1 as too severe, option 2 as too self-important and option 4 as too spineless. Option 3 seemed to be the best bet and this was the one I followed.

My own client was upset and told the story to several of the other candidates, all of whom she knew well in the closely connected world in which she was moving. In her view, this incident damaged the validity of the whole recruitment and selection exercise, because it suggested that the company running the assessments did not have sufficient understanding of the instruments to use them properly or else were too lazy to bother. My client might even have considered taking the case to an Employment Tribunal (wisely, she didn't). All the people she talked to are now in senior jobs where they are likely to employ consultants on selection exercises. They would be crazy not to have ruled this company out of the running. My guess is that the commissioning client will have got to hear about the episode. A company that could allow such a practice might well have sloppy quality controls, or be behaving in other unethical ways. As a commissioning client I would not want to risk my own reputation being sullied by any association with them.

What this story shows is that it's a smaller and better-informed world than you may think. This company avoided public exposure by the skin of its teeth. Ethical misdemeanours do mean that there is often a financial price to pay.

In a nutshell, values, purpose and ethics all affect your bottom line. The connections may not be immediately clear, but coaches who act without values, without clear and morally positive purpose and without stoutly defended ethics will soon find themselves without a business.

Quality service to clients

Thirty years of research into the sustainability of profitable businesses shows with utter clarity that customer service matters every bit as much as the quality of the product. In fact it matters critically when the sector or industry is highly competitive, as coaching now is.

You may think that we all provide wonderful service as a given. Unfortunately I don't think this is as true as we might all like to think. These are some recent examples of failed service gathered either directly from clients disappointed by what they had received from other practices or from assessing the portfolios of our Diploma candidates:

Emails remaining unanswered.

Unwillingness to compromise on contractual details – for instance insisting that the client either bought eight 90-minute sessions or none.

Abruptly terminating the coaching when a client failed to do her 'homework' and not listening to the perfectly reasonable explanation.

Promises that supervision tapes were 'in the post' but, like the cheque that somehow gets delayed, they weren't.

A coach who insisted on starting every session with deep breathing exercises in spite of the client's protests.

No proper recorded message on a phone, just the pleasant voice of the 1571 service.

Scruffy-looking documentation.

A letter containing both grammatical and spelling errors.

A client's name misspelt.

Letters that should have been tailored to the client but were clearly pro-formas that contained inappropriate detail.

The business value of high-quality service

Research into customer service comes down to a number of unsurprising conclusions.

When you have a reputation for high-quality service you are far more likely to have a high customer retention rate – in coaching this would mean that gatekeepers such as HR professionals will go on recommending you. You make greater gains than your competitors from word-of-mouth recommendation and have a bigger market share. Unsurprisingly, you attract and retain better-quality staff. In coaching terms this would mean that if and when you hire a PA or work with associates, they are likely to be higher calibre people than those attracted by a competitor offering inferior service. Also, good staff leave through disenchantment or shame when they see poor service happening around them. Finally, retaining even as few as 5 per cent of customers can increase profitability by as much as 25 per cent.

You may be thinking that little of this applies to you, if you are still at the stage of operating solo. But think again. It makes no difference when you are the customer whether the service provider is a sole trader or the representative of a big company. Over-promising and under-performing is endemic in small company service providers and as coaches we need to make sure that we do not fall into the same traps where our businesses are concerned.

It is helpful to think about what you promise your customer under four headings:

1 Product

This is the nature of your actual coaching: not the subject of this book. However, like any other product or service, your coaching must be at the leading edge of practice to attract customers. When a service feature is an innovation, it may provide a competitive advantage for a short time – but only until competitors catch up. A lot of coaches ask me whether they should invest money in acquiring further qualifications such as an MA, or in skills and disciplines such as NLP, Transactional Analysis, Psycho-Synthesis or psychometric instruments. You can be an excellent coach without any of these, but be aware that many of your competitors will probably have at least two of these sets of qualifications. When this becomes widespread, as with any business, it is no longer a competitive advantage to have them, but it may be a disadvantage to be without them.

It is important to benchmark your practice. Record sample coaching sessions and discuss them with a supervisor or just with a peer. Go to conferences and note how other coaches describe their work. Gather information from clients who have experienced other coaches. These are ways of finding out if your practice is as good as you claim when it is matched against what other coaches do. You can't afford not to invest in continuous training and development, especially if you are working solo. It is so easy to slip slowly out of date and not to know.

2 People skills

Let's take it for granted that the people skills associated with your own coaching are first class. But this part of the customer service ethic is about the total experience clients have in their contacts with you and anyone else associated with you. Essentially, the principles here are that every client is treated as an individual and that rapport is quickly created. The essence of rapport is respect and acceptance. So if you are looking to hire a serviced office, one principle by which you could choose would be the way you yourself are treated as a client. A warm welcome, the offer of refreshment, a willingness to take messages and swift, courteous service should all be part of the deal.

3 Presentation

Presentation refers to tangibles: the immediate impact of both the surroundings of your actual coaching room and the building it is in, the state of the equipment you use and the impression your print materials and website create (Chapter 4).

4 Processes

The operational aspect of running a coaching practice can be difficult if you are literally a sole trader with no back-up. I learnt this early on when my clients began to hint that it was becoming tortuously difficult to get a message to me and that I often seemed to go to ground for weeks. The reason was that my attention was wholly on doing the actual coaching, my client list was growing fast and I had temporarily forgotten that efficiency is what clients expect as a basic. Clients will judge you on how easy it is to make or alter a date, turn around an email message, return a phone call or receive the handouts that you promised them in your session. Many people deeply dislike voicemail and many will ring off rather than leave a message. A friendly up-to-date voicemail message, ideally renewed daily, will encourage them to leave the message. An actual human being answering the phone is even better.

Moments of truth

This concept refers to the moment in bull-fighting when the matador and the bull come face to face and there is just a split second when the outcome will be decided. All service industries have their moments of truth. The concept was popularized by Jan Carlsson, then CEO of SAS, the Scandinavian airline, who famously identified what they were for the airline industry and then stood with a stopwatch in the airport or on the plane, timing how long each moment of truth lasted. For an airline they were:

booking the ticket;

arriving at the airport;

checking in;

getting on the plane;

being served food and drink;

recovering baggage on arrival.

What Carlsson highlighted was how short each interaction was, sometimes shorter than a minute, yet it had the power to shape the relationship of the customer with the airline and to influence whether or not that customer rebooked. Every sector has its moments of truth and coaching is no different. Each actual coaching session has its own moments of truth, beyond our scope here. But the other moments of truth are not unlike those of the airline industry:

making an initial inquiry, either in person or through the website;

booking a date;

arriving at the coach's premises;

being served refreshments;

leaving.

While the quality of the actual coaching session will probably outweigh the impact of the more process-driven side of the encounter, we should never underestimate how quickly we can lose a client's goodwill:

The coach couldn't afford to hire rooms because he told me was still finishing his training, so we met in a terrible café place with shiny floors, shiny walls and shiny tables. We had to shout over the resulting clatter, including waiters coming to clear things away and then feeling awkward because we might have overstayed our welcome. I didn't like to comment on it because I was getting my coaching for a knock-down price, but I would actually have paid more for the sake of a better room.

The person taking my message was distinctly grumpy as if I was a nuisance and shouldn't have been ringing.

The coaching room was cold and I couldn't concentrate in the end because I was sure my nose was turning blue.

Nasty cheap mug, carelessly served and with coffee likely to drip over my clothes unless I fished out a tissue from my bag.

My coach was a cat person and we met in her home. I'm allergic to cat hair. She never noticed me snuffling but in the end I had to say something.

Getting it right will not ensure that your client rates the actual coaching, but thoughtful little touches can certainly increase the overall feel of being treated with respect and kindness:

The coaching room was great: not luxurious but had a peaceful calm atmosphere and I noticed there was no phone – I used to feel myself steadying down the minute I stepped into it. I could see that he had given it a lot of thought.

I really loved it that he always had a cappuccino from the sandwich bar next door waiting for me. I thought that was a nice personal touch.

Phone-answerer had a slight American-South accent, very courteous and friendly, called me Ma'am which I thought was cute and repeated the message back to me totally accurately so I felt absolutely sure that it would land.

I like it that my coach includes a bit of personal news in her emails to me – not too much because I know it's about my agenda not hers, but I respond to this – it makes me feel special.

I appreciated her just remembering to ask discreetly if I needed to go to the loo before we started or after we finished – perhaps she knows that we gentlemen over 50 are likely to need to do this!

When something goes wrong: service recovery

As with every other aspect of client service, you need a policy to guide your practice when something goes wrong. Do not think that your service is so impeccable that nothing will ever go wrong. It will. Of course you must aim for *zero-defects*, as the Quality gurus say, but sooner or later there will be a mishap or, much harder to detect, the low rumble of something that isn't quite right. The question is what to do when it occurs. Here are some common service disasters:

> The coach has been double booked and two clients arrive simultaneously.

> The coach is sitting in a tunnel on (name any line on the London Underground system), or on the M25 inside the biggest traffic jam that year, while the client is sitting in the coaching room waiting for her.

> The client has misread the date for the session on the email and arrives to find an empty coaching room.

> The client decides that the coaching is a waste of his time.

> The client blames the coach for the fact that she did not get the job she wanted.

> The client's PA sweeps off in a sulk without telling him that his session time had been changed.

> The firm's server is hijacked in cyber–space by a gang of amoral hackers who have used it to send disgusting porn to thousands of addresses and you are then banned by your ISP from sending or receiving email for a week while this is sorted out, giving an impression of inefficiency to clients who had sent emails and thought you were ignoring them

> ... and so on.

All of the above have happened to us over the years. The typical human response to a complaint is either aggressive self-defence or garrulous apologizing. Aggression comes from indignation if we feel we are in the right – or guilty anger if we know we have been caught out. The passive response of cringing, confessing all and agreeing that we are totally blameworthy comes from shame or fear. None of these responses will achieve what must be your aim in these circumstances: *service recovery*. Service recovery means that you maximize your chances of keeping that client's business.

There is a high cost to pay for failing to handle these difficulties skilfully. Research over the years has consistently shown that for every customer who makes a complaint, there are six or seven others who don't bother. Dissatisfied customers tell on average 10 people about their experience, while satisfied customers tell only half of that number. This is distressing for the service provider, but a disaster makes for a more dramatic story than a success.

When you fail to handle the complaint to that client's satisfaction, the chances of their returning are minute. When you handle it well – that is to say promptly and skilfully – at least eight out of ten customers are likely to return.

Dissatisfied customers most often don't complain and the reason is that they believe they will not be heard. They would rather take their custom elsewhere than risk humiliation or the emotional turmoil of making the complaint.

Handling complaints

There are two ideals: first to think through your systems to minimize the chances of mistakes and misunderstandings. This is why it is vital to be as clear as possible about what to expect on both sides before the work starts and as it continues. It is also why it is imperative to think through your standards. The best way to do this is to be guided by what your clients say they want – and appreciate once they have found it – and to keep checking the quality of your own services against what competitors are doing.

The second ideal is to solicit complaints. It takes courage because we'd all much rather hear how wonderful we are than to hear a criticism. By stressing that we really do want to hear thoughtful feedback we make it explicit that we care about the quality of what we provide. If any client does have a niggle, you will know about it immediately and at first hand rather than much later and at fifth hand, when it could have been distorted out of all recognition. This is why it is vital to ask for honest feedback from clients at every session, to hold frequent review meetings with clients when you are involved in a big contract and also why regular questionnaires are so informative.

All these tactics give clients the opportunity to complain as well as to praise. When you do this you will get invaluable opportunities to learn from clients – and to adjust your practices and systems accordingly. For instance, five years ago we had a run of embarrassing diary botch-ups and realized that our practice had expanded beyond the stage where it was acceptable to run a pencil and paper appointments book of the sort typically designed to serve a GP practice. A tailored electronic system has now made our appointments system as idiot-proof as possible, accessible remotely by any coach and automatically sending the coach an email when any date is added or changed.

On the occasions, fortunately rare, when there has been some other kind of error, our policy is

1   Establish the facts.
2   Find out what led up to it happening. This is not always obvious and you do not want to fall into the trap of assuming that fault lies with the last person in the chain on either side.
3   Stay utterly non-defensive. Spend twice as much time listening as talking.
4   Accept responsibility immediately where it is clear that the mistake lies on your side. We have a positively-no-blame culture in our company on the understanding that every mistake will tell us

something about what needs to improve. This means that when any of us gets something wrong, we own up immediately and will always apologize to the client – or each other – in person and graciously. Admin staff don't hide behind coaches and coaches don't hide behind admin staff.

5   Where you are working with a PA or a partner, trust them to sort it out promptly and on their own.

6   Never blame the client – even if it is apparent that the error lies on their side. Accept now and for ever the rule, No One Ever Won an Argument With a Customer. Note that this is not the same as saying that the customer is always right, because there are many occasions when the customer is plain wrong.

7   Use your rapport skills, so where a client is shouting (extremely rare, but it can happen), match his volume and energy. If you stay too calm you will merely inflame their anger.

8   Encourage clients to express any emotion they feel. It is essential to realize that you are not a personal target. Set aside any indignation you feel, even if the client is behaving rudely. The key skill here is to remain utterly detached while you are also sympathetic. Summarize, summarize, summarize – that tells the client that you have been listening. Just letting the client discharge any anger is often enough. When a complaint gets dragged out it is usually because the complainant feels she has not been heard.

9   Only at the later stage of the conversation put your side of things: you were at the mercy of the London Transport system, your partner was gravely ill, you could not get a signal on your mobile, the baby has kept you up five nights in a row – or you just forgot. Honesty pays. Or if you know you are not to blame and that the error probably arose on the client's side, explain what proof you have that your system is, in this case, robust, without accusing the client of the mistake.

10 Express your wish to sort it out and to keep the client's goodwill: *I'd really like us to sort this out so that we get back on track in a positive way.*

11 Ask, *What can we/I do to put this right?* As a coach you will know what a powerful question this is. It gives clients the chance to unload any further annoyance but, much more importantly, gives the control back to them. Most frequently, the answer will be, *Nothing – I feel fine now I've said it!*, or a rueful, *Well, these things happen.*

12 Our rule when we have seriously inconvenienced a client is to offer a free session. For minor errors we send a written apology and complimentary copies of books.

Just as stores refund or replace – but judiciously – so it is with complaints. You are bound at some stage to encounter a *vexatious complainant* – the kind of person who makes a career out of complaining, often inflating his complaints beyond what is fair – or merely whingeing out of a general belief that he is one of life's victims. In such cases you need to remain courteous and sympathetic but to stand firm, explaining why you cannot refund or go along with what you believe to be an unreasonable request. Here you will need to balance any reputational damage you believe such a person might do against your own indignation at potentially being conned.

Even in cases where you cannot immediately do what a complainant wants, the aim will be, as it always is in handling complaints, to deal with it immediately, to part on good terms and to aim for the classic win–win outcome. Failing that, look for one where even if neither has got what they want, both sides are able to walk away with their dignity intact.

Quality assurance through surveys

When you bid for larger contracts, it is normal practice to be asked how you maintain quality standards. One of the best ways of replying is to be able to say that you conduct regular client surveys. It is always better for this kind of survey to be done by a third party. This is because clients will tend to give you, the service-provider, the answer they believe you want to hear. So when you do this kind of interview yourself, you are unlikely to hear the entire truth as that client sees it. This is because clients will not wish to hurt and they may believe that the 'right' answer is to approve of what you do. This may be particularly true when they have chosen you personally, so any criticism may seem to reflect poorly on their own judgement. Also, you may not be able to hear criticisms because so much of your identity is tied up in belief in your own competence and hearing a criticism threatens that belief.

Where both these features are present – and it is likely that they often will be – a blandly meaningless and reassuring message is the most likely result. If so, then you might just as well not have bothered.

My advice is to offer this service to a fellow coach in return for their carrying out the same useful service for you. When you have a co-supervision arrangement, this could form the substance of several supervision sessions.

A draft questionnaire for clients

The best way to run this process is to do it by telephone. If that is too difficult, then a postal or emailed questionnaire will do, but you are less likely to get the complete frankness that talking and probing can provide. Here is one possible protocol. I first met an early version of it through the invaluable advice given to my then training department at the BBC by Mike Scally, based on his book with Barrie Hopson, *12 Steps to Success Through Service*, and have yet to find anything which beats its simplicity and ability to penetrate into the corners of a client's mind. It assumes a telephone format. Adapt accordingly if you are doing it by post or email.

> Introduce yourself and explain why you are doing the survey. Fix a date and time in advance, explaining that the interview will take 20 minutes. Reassure the client that she does not need to do any advance preparation.

> At the appointed time and date, double check that the client has the time to talk to you.

> If you are the third party, ask if you may quote the client directly to the coach and encourage him to agree to this. If he demurs, guarantee non-attributable confidentiality.

> Write down everything that the client says.

---

1 What services do I/XYZ Coaching provide for you?

Note: optional question when you are interviewing a client who has bought coaching from you and there is no ambiguity about the likely answer. However, for other clients this may seem a question with an obvious answer, but how clients describe it and what you think you are providing can be two different things.

2 How would you describe the quality of those services?

Poor/moderate/OK/outstanding

3 What criteria do you use when judging the quality of those services?

Note: you are looking here for the client's critical success factors (CSFs). These virtually always embrace

> speed of response;
> product or service matching client's needs;
> cost;
> flexibility.

Probe for clarity here by asking for specifics if the client uses generalizations such as 'understands my work'. When you get this kind of reply, ask *What evidence would you have that the coach understood your work?*

---

4 How would you prioritize those criteria – which would come first/last for you?

5 How would you rate me/XYZ Coaching against those criteria?

6 What other sources of coaching services do you have?

7 What advice would you give me/XYZ Coaching about improving my/their service?

8 What would cause you to switch to another supplier?

9 What's coming up in your work/the organization that could change what you need form me/XYZ Coaching?

10 Finally, what might I/they do that would improve the relationship you have with me/XYZ Coaching?

Surveying a minimum of ten clients should give you reliable results. Where you have an established practice, select clients who represent a fair sample of your list. In your first year, it would be good practice to survey all your clients.

When you have finished the interviews:

What themes emerge?

What do clients particularly like?

What specific grumbles might you need to address immediately?

How can you follow up the answers to question 9 – the question that gives you valuable insight into how the client might need your services in the future?

As a parallel process, check your quality systems by filling in this worksheet

Key
1 = yes/excellent/all the time
2 = so-so/moderate/some of the time
3 = room for improvement

	1 √	2 √	3 √

Product/services
My standards are defined by my clients
I benchmark my standards against those of my competitors
I measure my quality standards
In my last financial year
 	
    I undertook at least two days of training
    I attended one conference with other coaches
    I had at least four supervision sessions
 	
I asked an experienced coach to review at least two recorded sessions with me			

People skills
Everyone who comes into contact with my clients on my premises or on the phone
 	
    Welcomes them warmly
    Treats them as a valued individual
    Has discretion to act alone to sort out problems
    Sorts out problems quickly and efficiently
    Offers them appropriate refreshment, if face to face
    Understands the link of their work to our joint success			

Presentation
My print materials and website say what I want them to say about me and my work
The building containing my coaching room is appropriate for the work I do
My coaching room is
 	
    Immaculately presented
    Comfortable to sit in for long periods
    Private
    Quiet, guaranteed no interruptions
    Pleasantly furnished			

Processes Clients can contact me easily I have minimal dependence on voicemail			

	1 √	2 √	3 √
I return emails and phone calls within 48 hours My appointments system is reliable My letters and emails are appropriately tailored for each client Invoices are accurate and dispatched speedily My tax is paid on time I pay suppliers promptly I have a consistent system for the documentation involved in the first and last stages of the coaching process Debtor days (the average number of days during which anyone owes you money) are no greater than 30 Materials are dispatched promptly			

Feedback
I have conducted a client questionnaire
 	
   Within the last year
   Carried out by a third party
 	
I ask for client feedback at every coaching session
I ensure that any partners or associates ask for client feedback at every session
It is easy for clients to complain
I log and deal with complaints or negative feedback promptly
I retain clients who have complained			

TOTALS			

Mostly 1s: You must be running a highly efficient and effective practice. What do you need to do to ensure that you maintain these high standards?

Mostly 2s: Where are the strengths? What do you need to do to sustain them? Is there one area of weakness that stands out? If so, how can you address it?

Mostly 3s: A big agenda for change. It will be easier to tackle it with help. Where could you find such help?

Brand

Brand is a recognizable and distinctive feature of a business and has enormous value when it is positive. When you choose a low-cost airline rather than British Airways, you are positively choosing the no-frills service of one brand over the higher cost and more luxurious service of another. When customers buy designer jeans rather than the bargain-basement copy obtainable at a chain store, it is because they believe that the mysteriously desirable quality of the designer brand makes it worth paying several thousand per cent more in price.

I like the metaphor of a healthy tree to describe brand. The roots are your core purpose and they support everything else. The trunk is your values and ethics. Without strong roots and trunk, the tree will wither and die. The branches are made up of what the marketing experts call the Marketing Mix. One version is another handy acronym – the 6 Ps:

Product or service – your coaching.

Place – where you do it.

Price – what you charge.

People – your skills and those of the people working with you.

Positioning – where you are pitched in your market place.

Promotion – what you say about yourself, where and how you say it and sell it.

The blossom or fruit on the tree is your brand: it is the product of everything else, contains the seeds for future growth and, like blossom, it can be fragile, easily destroyed in harsh weather or by pests.

Sometimes you find there's nothing in these brand promises at all

All commercial organizations have a brand and all chase the chimera of brand loyalty, that elusive goal which will ensure that customers go on choosing you over the competition. Along with brand loyalty goes the equally useful concept of *brand promise*. What, essentially, do you promise your customers? How would *you* sum it up? What would *they* say about why they choose you rather than a competitor? Nothing damages you more quickly than a customer discovering that your brand promise is empty – that is there is discrepancy between what you say about yourself and what clients actually experience.

Brand percolates every aspect of your interaction with clients: what you offer, how you describe it, how you promote it and how customers experience you face to face.

Absolute essentials

- What's your purpose/mission?
- What core values will you demonstrate in your business?
- What simple quality checks do you commit to – for instance, making it a rule to ask for feedback at every coaching session?
- How would you describe your brand?
- What is your brand promise?
- What are you doing to ensure its consistency and health?

---

7 The Future

Your business is thriving. You have made more money than you ever dreamed was possible and have exceeded the forecast in your business plan for this year. Your order book is full. In fact it's too full and you are beginning to fret about whether you will be able to take a holiday. You notice that far from greeting the prospect of a new client with delight, it fills you with a dreadful sense of oppression. You are drained and irritable. You begin to resent clients – for goodness sake, they are so demanding, why won't they leave you alone!

When your offer is one that people want, when your coaching skills, your promotional material, your customer service and your selling techniques are all outstandingly good, you cannot but succeed. It is at this point that success may overwhelm you. This chapter considers two related topics: whether or not it is a good idea to expand your business and the future of coaching generally.

It is actually extremely difficult to keep a business at the same size for any length of time. Here is why.

The success scenario
You do well – very well. Word of mouth begins to spread news of your excellent work. Your marketing materials reinforce the message. This will take a few years, but if your business continues to be just you, it will create the situation with which I opened this chapter. What happens then? One option is that you continue to drive yourself on, accepting every new client, maybe seeing four clients for two-hour sessions on many days of the week and possibly spreading into weekends as well. You will know that this is too many. But fear that this will be the last piece of work you ever get is endemic in a small business – you can't quite believe that success will continue. In the loss of perspective which this frame of body and mind involves, because by then you are physically and mentally exhausted, you continue to say *yes* to all of it.

Sooner rather than later, the quality of your work begins to suffer. You find it difficult to concentrate fully in your coaching sessions. There are muddles about dates. You forget to send clients the materials you promised. Clients don't seem to get to their outcomes as quickly as they used to. They pick up faint threads of your resentment about the demands they are making on your energy and skill. They are no longer so enthusiastic about you. At the same time, the sheer pressure of a full diary begins to force you to turn clients away. In a relatively short time, the clients who could have recommended you are warning prospective clients that you are *always busy*, or *overbooked*, so some people don't bother to contact you. The technical term for what has happened is *over-trading*. You have taken your business beyond what it can sustain and rapid collapse is inevitable unless you take action a long time before things get to crisis.

The failure scenario
It seems to be taking for ever for your business to develop. You are bored by the admin side and especially dislike the promotional side. You wait for word of mouth to grow your reputation, and it is happening – but slowly, slowly. Financial pressure is an issue. It all feels disheartening. A sense of disappointment creeps into your work. You begin to wonder whether you are cut out for coaching, even though in your heart you know you are good at it, but clients begin to discern your lack of confidence. What happens next depends on how ruthless you are able to be about where the problems lie. In fact your best bet is some outside help – for instance from a fellow coach who specializes in small businesses.

Expand – or shrink?

The minuses of growth

The main minus is cost and the risks associated with it. It is expensive to employ staff: not only do they need a roof over their heads, they also need computers and phones, you must arrange for tax to be deducted, salaries to be paid and their statutory rights observed. You have to feel confident that the business can sustain the overheads involved. If you have ever watched the hard work of parent birds feeding the gaping mouths of their young, you will know just how they feel. When a consulting or coaching business fails, one of the main reasons is that ambition ran ahead of reality: an over-expensive office was hired or too many people taken on. Growth is not a step to take when your revenue stream is uncertain but it may be an essential one at the point where you land your first or second big contract. Remember that part-time work is an attractive option to many people and if you are feeling cautious, this may be a good first step into acquiring staff.

However careful you are about hiring, it is all too easy to make a mistake. Correcting a poor-quality selection decision is expensive, not just in actual money but also in possible reputation damage and disappointment all round. Putting it right is time- and energy-consuming.

For many small business owners there is also the necessity to let your baby grow up and this can be harder than you think. Other people may challenge your cherished ideas and you can longer be in control of absolutely every aspect of how things are done. Furthermore, your own role will change. At some point you will have to decide whether you want to go on just being a coach, whether you should combine this with a managerial role or hire a specialist. No business will manage itself. Someone has to run it, though not necessarily full time, and this is a different skill-set from the cluster that is involved in being a coach.

At the critical early growth point for Management Futures we had merged our business with that of Phil Hayes. Phil and I were clear that we did not want to take these managerial duties on. Fortunately, help was at hand in the shape of my husband Alan who had been a partner in the enterprise from the start. Alan has had the best part of a whole career as a senior manager. He eagerly embraced the role of leading the finance, marketing, business development and operational aspects of the company, much to the relief of everyone else. As a business grows, specialization of roles is inevitable and it is essential to have proper professional management.

The plusses of growth

A bigger business makes a more confident impact on the world. It looks more serious. You are able to tell clients overtly that you are in it for the long term and not just playing at something which could disappear tomorrow. In this way growth can generate more growth. US research shows convincingly that bigger consulting and coaching businesses build faster, are more profitable, spend longer periods with each client and can charge higher fees than one-person practices.

It may be possible to work from home for a while, but after a bit, the intrusion into your domestic privacy can be overwhelming. For our first five years, we ran the business from home. Fortunately this was a forgiving London house, built in 1826, which, in its colourful history, had seen over-crowding before, though maybe not of this sort. But soon we got to the stage of realizing that twenty people possessed copies of our keys. Literally every room except our bedroom and bathroom had a computer and printer and every landing was stacked with storage boxes. We had also just won our first major contract. So it was clear that we had to move to proper offices. Unsurprisingly, this was the point at which the business took off – doubling turnover within 18 months. It was exciting, but at the point of making the decision, it also felt risky to take on a five-year lease.

When there are several coaches in the same practice, it allows for a degree of specialization and for a balancing of strengths and weaknesses, or for developing individual interests. For instance, there may be one coach who enjoys the selling aspect of developing a business, or one who enjoys addressing conferences. It is pleasant to have colleagues with whom to exchange ideas. It makes it less likely that your ideas will become stale and more likely that you will develop new products and services in response to market needs. When business is either slack or over-busy, there is someone else to share the responsibility. When you have admin support, assuming you make the right appointment, you immediately improve the human face and efficiency of your operation.

Finally, when you grow a successful business, it has capital value and may be saleable, if and when you decide that you and your partners want to move on to something else.

Alternatives

Fortunately it's not just a black/white, right/wrong set of choices. There are flexible alternatives and all have something to be said for them.

Associateship

Whether as the person doing the hiring or as the person who is being hired, there is much to be said for the associate relationship. As an associate you are a freelance, working as and when the other partner in the relationship cannot resource a project themselves. There are a number of ways in which this arrangement can work. The most common is that the associate is simply paid on an hourly, daily or per project basis. Another is that the associate is guaranteed a certain number of days per year in return for a first-refusal promise of work.

As the person taking on the associate:

You have only short-term responsibility for the associate: you do not have to pay her tax and insurance. You can stay light-footed yourself, responding to what the market needs without any of the worries associated with full-time employees.

You can expand the range of specialisms you offer to clients.

You can offer associates more work if they turn out to be high performers or lose interest in them if they are not.

Be clear about the business ethics you expect, not least that if a client who comes to the associate through your marketing effort then in turn generates further recommendations, you expect the work to be carried out on associate terms.

But, bear in mind that:

> It's a two-way relationship. Associates appreciate a business relationship that is steady. If you want to attract loyalty, there will need to be something in it for the other party. Being offered fair rates, being included, made to feel welcome, being offered training at reduced or nil cost are other possible benefits that may make it worth a high-quality associate choosing you rather than another practice.

> Outstanding performers will be able to earn more under their own flag and for this reason alone will usually put the needs of their own business before the needs of yours, or may be able to get better rates from another practice. They may not be available when you want them.

As the associate:

> You have flexibility – you can say yes or no depending on whether you like the sound of the work. There is no obligation to do your share of work that others regard as boring or unpleasant.

> You work with others and get to feel part of a team: valuable if you find too much solo activity tedious.

> It is a painless way of keeping up to date: for instance you may be offered supervision as part of the deal.

> You do not have responsibility for marketing: that effort and cost is borne by the person taking you on. For this reason alone, becoming an associate is attractive to coaches.

> You potentially gain access and more quickly to a wider range of clients than you could achieve alone and are therefore likely to increase your skill and marketability.

But bear in mind that:

> It's a two-way relationship. Practices appreciate loyalty and willingness to muck in. Where the relationship becomes too transactional or if it looks as if all you are interested in is the money, that is where ultimately the relationship will break down. Think about what you can bring as well as what you want to take.

You may have to manage your resentment that the fee at which you are charged out is anything from twice to one third more than you actually receive.

You may feel second best compared to people who are in full-time employment with the practice.

For all these reasons, the associate relationship is more fragile than one based on full-time employment. There is less commitment on both sides. Drifting apart is easy. The potential for misunderstanding is always there. For instance, what looked like a promising partnership with another, smaller, practice came to grief when they sent us what felt like a huge invoice, citing the large number of days they said had gone into the work. We looked at their output and felt pretty sure that we could have done the same thing in half the time. With both sides feeling jumpy and exploited about what, after all, was a delicate and temporary-feeling relationship, this could only end in tears – and did.

We take the business of choosing associates seriously and as time has gone on are increasingly aware that it is a process needing careful husbandry on both sides. We make tougher demands for experience, knowledge and qualifications than we did in earlier years and this is matched by associates making bolder demands on us. We start cautiously with a small project and assess how it has gone from both sides. Like any other worthwhile relationship, the associate partnership needs work and commitment all round.

Consortia

Here is yet another variant. A group of coaches gets together to bid for a particular project, or to pilot the idea of working together more formally over a longer period. There is no legal basis to the partnership: each is a separate business, but acts as one for purposes of marketing. This has all the pluses and minuses of associate relationships except that there is no Principal to absorb costs or act as a decision-maker. For this reason alone, all concerned need to have high levels of conflict-resolution skills. If you are attracted to this idea, it is essential to look all around the potential gains and pitfalls. Before you even put pen to paper in a bid, have frank discussions about:

what the longer-term future could be for the consortium;

what you are looking for in the other partner(s); which values you need to share and what they will mean in practice;

who will do what and how they will be rewarded – e.g. for time spent writing proposals and other indirect ways of earning income;

how you will log and charge expenses to the project;

how you will monitor quality;

how you will handle the resulting conflict if one person is more popular or successful with clients than the other.

Outsourcing

This can work with any of the above arrangements. You decide that you are far too small to have your own marketing expert, finance expert or PR person. You hire in the help you need, either just for yourself or, probably more sensibly, for a consortium of other coaches. The discussion on page 51 of how to choose a designer for your website is an example of outsourcing in practice.

Branching out into products

In coaching, you are selling your time, so if you are not working directly with clients, you are not earning. As your business grows, you may want to consider adding products to your coaching services. These can be sold through your website as a supporting act for your coaching or as an additional marketing tool. The possibilities here include conventional books, e-books, tapes, audio books and DVDs. Where you develop a bank of handout material, it may lend itself to further development as a book, or as the foundation for an instructional audio book.

Think about what your purpose is in creating a product. For instance, a book may add substance to any claims you make about expertise in your subject. An audio book may be a way of gaining new clients because if someone buys an audio book they may also be in the market for coaching on the same topic. Some products arise simply out of frustration that you want to give some kind of follow-up material to clients and you discover that there is nothing suitable available. My own books on the Myers Briggs Type Indicator, with profiles on the 16 Types in a work context, developed out of just such a frustration: I found British clients resistant to the US language of the Consulting Psychologists Press materials, excellent though they are. I began what turned, somewhat to my surprise, into a major research and development project. This eventually resulted in two books and a disk/CD. These all sell well, creating significant income streams for us, the disk/CD because it is a high-price/low-volume item selling to other coaches and the books because they are low-price/high-volume items selling well in multiple copies to the clients of those coaches.

Be ruthless about the probable demand and about your own ability to produce something that your market is likely to want, otherwise you may just be embarking on an expensive piece of vanity publishing.

Be aware that when you make a decision to introduce a product you are entering a different market with different competitors so all the same considerations about what you offer, its price, its benefits and its target buyer will apply, just as they do to coaching. The development cost can be high because it is essential to have professional help in production, design and packaging. Home-made looks just that and is best avoided. Remember to factor-in the cost of marketing, storage and dispatch and be realistic about how many copies you would need to sell before breaking even.

The future of coaching

This section sums up themes I have touched on elsewhere in this book. In order to consider the future of your business you will need to take a view on how the whole profession is likely to develop.

One sign of growing interest in the field is that coaching is increasingly the target of sceptical articles written by journalists, some of whom see it as another way for the *self-help industry*, as they call it, to exploit vulnerable people. This is similar to the way therapy was attacked in the 1980s and the grounds of the attacks are also similar and similarly contradictory

Coaches have no actual wisdom, they are just out for themselves.

It's all platitudinous: they wrap up common sense in jargon.

Coaches are dangerous: they tell people to leave their partners or make radical changes in their lives when they don't understand all the issues.

Coaches encourage people to see themselves as victims – people are paying to be heard while they whinge.

Why don't people just phone a friend? They could get the same advice for free.

Anyone consulting a life coach is probably unsophisticated and to be pitied. Alternatively it's a sign of pathetic self-absorption – the sort of thing that D-list celebrities do. It's the equivalent of the worried-well coming to consult a GP.

Life coaching is just another way for people with serious mental health problems to get therapy without owning up to it.

Where executive coaching is concerned the attacks have a similar flavour to attacks on management consultants where the classic joke is that a management consultant is someone who borrows your watch to tell you the time and then makes off with the watch. This public scrutiny is welcome and useful because it puts us on our toes. It also puts a premium on ethical, skilful PR and we all need to get better at doing this. It damages everyone when any individual coach or coaching company makes inflated claims for their coaching or positions it as the new snake-oil.

The popularity of life coaching is likely to continue, not least because anything worth attacking also looks interesting. Coaching has already become a standard part of many popular TV shows in the make-over genre, and although it may not be coaching as some of us would like it to be, the results can look impressive, thus generating more potential clients.

I believe that the coaching market will become much more differentiated than it is now. The signs are already there and I have drawn on them in Chapter 2. One of the most obvious differentiators now is life coaching from executive coaching. Within each of these there will be people who will find niche specialities. As clients become more aware of what coaching involves, they will increasingly look for people who can meet a closely targeted need. In our practice we can all deal with the normal range of executive clients' concerns about management, career and life issues. But we know where specialist expertise could add depth that an individual might lack. This is why we have people who specialize in job-search, voice, style, strategy, training, addiction – and many more. The way we handle it is that while any one of us will be, as it were, the base-coach for that client, we will refer the client to a colleague for some parts of their coaching.

As a result of this trend, I expect to see more alliances as small coaching practices merge. We could see a change such as that in the accountancy and consulting sectors where the industry is dominated by a few big players followed by a number of medium-sized firms and many thousands more of one- or two-person outfits fighting it out for what is left.

In the notable downturn in the consulting market a few years ago, many of the big firms saw coaching as a way of keeping going through difficult times. Having discovered it, they are unlikely to let it go. Consulting, coaching, facilitation and organizational development are increasingly likely to be bundled as part of the problem-solving techniques that consultancies offer to the organizational market.

As organizations take far more interest in coaching, their demands to cap costs will probably be unstoppable unless they are convinced that by paying top prices they are buying significantly more skill and experience. The consultancy market generally is over-populated and while any one individual coach or consultant is just a minnow compared with the big fish, when there are thousands of them their effect on the market can be considerable. This is why at the moment there is definitely downward pressure on fees. Even five years ago we were rarely asked how we would calculate Return On Investment (ROI), whereas now it is an increasingly frequent request at tender stage. You need to have answers to these questions, however tricky they are to answer.

Life-coaching could come to replace therapy as the first resort of troubled people. If this becomes part of the medical profession's understanding of how to treat low-risk but distressed patients or how to offer help for addictions, this could create yet more differentiation and more demands for accreditation.

All of this is leading to pressure for regulation. This is still a confused situation but the moves towards accreditation of *training courses* are strong, though this is a long way from accrediting individual coaches and an even longer way from making it impossible for an untrained and unaccredited coach to set up in business. But to be untrained or to be trained by a provider outside of the accreditation process is a commercial risk.

Starting and then developing a coaching practice takes talent, determination and business flair. It also takes time. When you stick at it, the rewards are immense, not just in money but in personal satisfaction. I close this book with a success story from Polly McDonald. Polly undertook our coaching course and Diploma. She had worked with notable success as a television producer and then as Managing Director of a large independent production company, so, as with many of us, coaching is a second career. She now works full time as a much-in-demand coach. Her story says it all: the effort it takes to overcome squeamishness at selling, the pay-off from investing in your own development and the immense satisfaction you achieve from doing work you love:

> *Polly McDonald*
> As a big birthday and the millennium approached, I realized I was not happy and wanted a change. Coaching was becoming recognized in the UK and appealed to me as a career where I could use my sponsoring and nurturing sides.
>
> I undertook an intensive coaching course and did some NLP training. I then realized there was the small issue of finding some clients! Though genuinely fired up about coaching, marketing was another matter entirely.
>
> Someone suggested I write to 100 people I knew. I managed 50. The response I got was: *Well done for getting out of telly, it's so ghastly now, you're SO brave, I wish I had the courage.* Lovely to hear but I didn't feel brave, no business was forthcoming and it clearly wasn't going to be that easy – oh dear. I realized that for 20 years, I'd been approached for almost every job I'd done. And now, horror of horrors, I was going to have to ASK PEOPLE FOR WORK. Nice girls don't ask, they wait to be asked . . . So, I stared at contact lists, became a world expert in displacement behaviour and my meagre savings dwindled. I picked up a few personal clients, mostly friends of friends.
>
> I realized writing and calling people once wasn't going to cut the mustard. I needed to be more tenacious, to talk a good fight about

who I was and what I did. One thing that really helped me here was allowing myself to know that even though I might sometimes feel like a worm, that was not how I was perceived by others. I was the brave woman who had found the courage to strike out on her own and been the MD of a successful company. Once I stepped into those shoes, it became easier to sell myself.

I proceeded to contact television companies and broadcasters, with limited success, but I knew by then that Rome wasn't built in a day. And so constantly reminding myself how I was seen by others, I screwed up my courage and kept going. I have now grown my practice and have a great balance of corporate and personal clients and I *love* my work.

I take my own personal development and learning seriously. Each year I do at least one big course and also attend evening and day events if they appeal. As well as giving me great personal pleasure, I gain new insights and tools. My clients also like this and are impressed by my commitment to my own learning.

And five years on, marketing is still something I'd rather not do, but I know that many of the most successful coaches are those who understand how crucial it is. After all, no one can give you work if they don't know you're there!

polly@alchemyalliance.com

Those of us in coaching now are pioneers. We have a long way to go and much to learn. But could any journey be more interesting or worthwhile? Here's to our joint success ...

Bibliography

Bacal, R. (2002) *The Complete Idiot's Guide to Consulting*. Madison, WI: Alpha Books with John A. Woods, CWL Publishing Enterprises.

Block, P. (1981) *Flawless Consulting*. San Diego, CA: Pfeiffer.

Bridges, W. (1997) *Creating You and Co; Be the Boss of Your Own Career*. London: Nicolas Brealey.

Buckingham, M. and Clifton, D. (2002) *Now Discover Your Strengths*. London: Simon and Schuster UK.

Collins, J.C. and Porras, J.I. (1996) *Built to Last*. London: Century, Random House.

Fairley, S.G. and Stout, C.E. (2004) *Getting Started in Personal and Executive Coaching*. Hoboken, NJ: John Wiley.

Holtz, H. (1994) *How to Succeed as an Independent Consultant*. Hoboken, NJ John Wiley and Sons.

Hopson, B. and Scally, M. (1991) *12 Steps to Success Through Service*. London: Mercury Books.

Morgen, S.D. (1997) *Selling With Integrity*. New York: Berkeley Books.

Morgen, S.D. (2003) *Buying Facilitation*. Austin, Texas: Morgen Publishing.

RoAne, S. (2000) *How to Work a Room*. New York: HarperCollins.

Rogers, J. (1998) *Sixteen Personality Types at Work in Organisations*. London: Management Futures; Milton Keynes: ASK Europe.

Rogers, J. (2004) *Coaching Skills: A Handbook*. Maidenhead: Open University Press, McGraw Hill Education.

Rogers, J. and Waterman, J. (1997). Palo Alto, CA: Consulting Psychologists Press.

Senge, P.M. (1992) *The Fifth Discipline*. London: Random Century Group.

Walker, K. , Ferguson, C. and Denvir, P. (1998) *Creating New Clients*. London and New York: Continuum.

Weiss, A. (1999) *Million Dollar Consulting: The Professional's Guide to Growing a Practice*. New York: McGraw-Hill.

Useful Websites

Businessballs.com: A free personal and organizational development website. Crisp, high-quality information, including a section on selling.

coachandgrowrich.com: Useful site with some free and some buyable materials for coaches.

Quickmba.com: A useful source for executive coaches of clear explanations of business terms and concepts.

Searchenginewatch.com: Advice on how to maximize the chances of getting your website listed by search engines.

Taxassist.co.uk: A source of tax and business advisers for small businesses.

Acknowledgements

My gratitude to all of the following:

The coaches who agreed to write short pieces for this book describing their experience. I have given their full names and contact details.

The coaches who agreed to be quoted anonymously and with their details disguised.

Chris Radley for the drawings on pages 87 and 89.

Mike Scally for permission to adapt materials from his work on customer service.

Sharon Drew Morgen for permission to adapt the diagram on page 89 and to draw on her ideas on selling (Chapter 5), though responsibility for their interpretation is mine.

My colleagues at Management Futures for their constant support and friendship, and especially to my husband Alan Rogers, who has shown us all what real business leadership means in building our company.

Your feedback on this book is welcome. Please email me with your comments and questions: jenny.rogers@managementfutures.co.uk or contact us through our website: www.managementfutures.co.uk

Index